BETWEEN FACT AND FICTION

Books by Edward Jay Epstein

BETWEEN FACT AND FICTION

THE PROBLEM OF JOURNALISM

Edward J. Epstein

VINTAGE BOOKS
A Division of Random House
New York

VINTAGE BOOKS EDITION, OCTOBER 1975

"The Panthers and the Police" and "Do You Sincerely Want to be Rich?" originally appeared in *The New Yorker*. "The Vietnam War: What Happened vs. What We Saw" was first published in three parts in *TV Guide*. "Truth and Journalism," "Did the Press Uncover Watergate?" "The Death of Lancelot to the Death of a President," and "Truth in the Courtroom" were originally published in *Commentary*.

Library of Congress Cataloging in Publication Data

Epstein, Edward J. 1935–
  Between Fact and Fiction.

  1. Journalism—the United States I. Title.
PN4867.E67   070.4'3   75–16421
ISBN 0–394–71396–6

Manufactured in the United States of America

TO
Edward C. Banfield
and
James Q. Wilson

CONTENTS

PREFACE

The essays in this book are all variations on a single theme—the problem of approaching truth in journalism. In evaluating the reporting of such phenomena as Watergate, the Black Panthers, the Pentagon Papers, the reopening of the investigation of the assassination of President John F. Kennedy, and the Vietnam war, I attempted to shed some light on the process by which information is gathered, edited, and presented to the public by the press and television. The case of Watergate, I suggest, illustrates the problem inherent in journalistic investigations; the case of the Black Panthers shows the vulnerability of the press to factual-sounding claims; the case of the Pentagon

Papers suggests that the editing process tends to reduce complex issues to simplistic themes of journalism; the assassination inquiry demonstrates, as do other essays, the almost total reliance of demagogues on the press—and vice versa—for the publication of sensational charges; and the essay on the coverage of the Vietnam war attempts to define the dependence of the television journalist on publicly accepted models of reporting. Television has provided a vital and distinctive element to journalism,* and in the essays on "the rating game," bias in TV news, and the televised Vietnam war, I attempt to show that there are distinctive requisites which give direction to this form of reporting news.

Most of these essays were written in Cambridge between 1967 and 1972, when I was attempting to live simultaneously in the antipodal worlds of political science and journalism. The discipline of political science demanded a focus on the typical and routine elements of political behavior, and an explanation based on policies, processes, and institutions which presumably underlay personal deeds. Journalism, on the other hand, focused on the atypical and extraordinary events, and sought explanation in personalities and anecdotes. While both disciplines might deal with the same subject, they would apply to it totally different logics. For example, when Daylight Saving Time was instituted by Congress in January 1974, newspapers, news magazines, and television news

---

*See my *News from Nowhere* (New York: Random House, 1974).

carried a rash of sensational stories about children being struck down by cars while going to school in the dark. (*Newsweek* alone listed four such bloody accidents.) The journalistic theme was that Daylight Saving Time was leading to the slaughter of schoolchildren, and that the reports presented in gory detail were confirming evidence. A political scientist, studying the same problem, inquired of the National Safety Council and found that twenty schoolchildren were killed in January of the preceding year; he concluded, therefore, that Daylight Saving Time had no appreciable effect on the safety of schoolchildren. I know of no way to resolve such tensions between the reporting procedures of social science and journalism, but have attempted to use the former as a special-purpose lens for examining the latter—despite the obvious fact that any lens contains its own distortions.

To the extent that these essays are successful, I am greatly indebted to my teachers, colleagues, and students at Harvard and M.I.T. In particular, these essays have benefited from the criticisms and comments of Allan A. Altshuler, Edward C. Banfield, Allan Bloom, Howard Darmstadter, Marc E. Green, Yaron Ezrari, Andrew Hacker, Paul Halpern, Jeremy Larner, Bruce Kovner, Seymour Martin Lipset, Daniel P. Moynihan, Ithiel de sola Poole, William Rothman, John Rubinstein, Paul Weaver, Suzanne Weaver, William Marslan Wilson, Deirdre Wilson, James Q. Wilson, and Cynthia Worswick.

These essays also benefited enormously from the time, patience, and advice given to me by my editors. Services well beyond the call of duty were rendered by Aaron Asher, John Berendt, Robert Bingam, Byron Dobell, Jason Epstein, John Foley, Joe Fox, Norman Podhoretz, Edward Thomas, Gerald Walker, William Whitworth, and Roger Youman.

Finally, I owe a special debt to William Shawn for first stimulating my interest in writing about the ways of journalism, and always encouraging that interest.

—E.J.E.

BETWEEN FACT AND FICTION

INTRODUCTION: JOURNALISM AND TRUTH

The problem of journalism in America proceeds from a simple but inescapable bind: journalists are rarely, if ever, in a position to establish the truth about an issue for themselves, and they are therefore almost entirely dependent on self-interested "sources" for the version of reality that they report. Walter Lippmann pointed to the root of the problem more than fifty years ago when he made a painful distinction between "news" and truth. "The function of news is to signalize an event; the function of truth is to bring to light the hidden facts, to set them into relation with each other, and make a picture of reality on which men can act." Because news-reporting and truth-seeking have different ultimate purposes, Lippmann postulated that "news" could be expected to coincide with truth in only a few limited areas, such as the scores of baseball games or elections, where the results are definite and measurable. In the more complex and ambiguous recesses of political life, where the outcome is almost always in doubt or dispute, news reports could not be expected to exhaust, or perhaps even indicate, the truth of the matter. This divergence between news and truth stemmed not from the inadequacies of newsmen but from the exigencies of the news business, which limited the time, space, and resources that could be allotted to any single story. Lippmann concluded pessimistically that if the public required a more truthful interpretation of the world they lived in, they would have to depend on institutions other than the press.

Contemporary journalists would have some difficulty accepting such a distinction between news and truth. Indeed, newsmen now almost invariably depict themselves not merely as reporters of the fragments of information that come their way, but as active pursuers of the truth. In the current rhetoric of journalism, "stenographic reporting," where the reporter simply but accurately repeats what he has been told, is a pejorative term used to describe inadequate journalism; "investigative reporting," on the other hand, where the reporter supposedly ferrets out a hidden truth, is an honorific enterprise to which all journalists are supposed to aspire. In the post-Watergate era, moreover, even critics of the press attribute to it powers of discovery that go well beyond reporting new developments.

Yet despite the energetic claims of the press, the limits of journalism described by Lippmann still persist in basically the same form. Individual journalists may be better educated and motivated today than they were fifty years ago, but newspapers still have strict deadlines, which limit the time that can be spent investigating a story; a restricted number of news "holes," which limit the space that can be devoted to elucidating the details of an event; and fixed budgets, which limit the resources that can be used on any single piece of reportage. Today, as when Lippmann wrote, "The final page is of a definite size [and] must be ready at a precise moment."

Under these conditions, it would be unreasonable to expect even the most resourceful journalist to produce anything more than a truncated version of reality. Beyond this, however, even if such restraints were somehow suspended, and journalists had unlimited time, space, and financial resources at their disposal, they would still lack the forensic means and authority to establish the truth about a matter in serious dispute. Grand juries, prosecutors, judges, and legislative committees can compel witnesses to testify before them—offering the inducement of immunity to reluctant witnesses and the threat of perjury and contempt actions to inconsistent witnesses; they can subpoena records and other evidence, and test it all through cross-examination and other rigorous processes. Similarly, scientists, doctors, and other experts can establish facts in a disputed area, especially when there is unanimous agreement on the results of a particular test or analysis, because their authority and technical expertise are ac-

cepted in their distinct spheres of competency.
Such authority derives from the individual reputation of the expert, certification of his *bona fides* by
a professional group which is presumed to have a
virtual monopoly of knowledge over the field, and
a clearly articulated fact-finding procedure (such
as was used, for instance, in establishing the eras-
ures on the Nixon tapes). Even in more problematic areas, such as the social sciences, academic researchers can resolve disputed issues.
Acceptance of such an academic verdict, however,
will depend heavily on the qualifications of the
researcher, the degree to which his sources are
satisfactorily documented, and the process of review by other scholars in the field through which,
presumably, objections to the thesis are articulated and errors corrected. In all cases, a
necessary (though not sufficient) condition for establishing the truth is the use of an acceptable
procedure for examining, testing, and evaluating
evidence.

　　Reporters possess no such wherewithal for
dealing with evidence. Unlike the judicial officer,
journalists cannot compel a witness to furnish
them an account of an event. Witnesses need only
tell reporters what they deem is in their own self-
interest, and then they can lie or fashion their
story to fit a particular purpose without risking
any legal penalty. Nor can a journalist test an
account by hostile cross-examination without
jeopardizing the future cooperation of the witness.
Indeed, given the voluntary nature of the relationship between a reporter and his source, a continued flow of information can only be assured if

the journalist's stories promise to serve the interest of the witness (which precludes impeaching the latter's credibility). In recent years, journalists have cogently argued that if they are forced to testify before grand juries about their sources, they will be cut off from further information. The same logic applies with equal force to criticizing harshly or casting doubts on the activities of these sources. The misreporting of a series of violent incidents involving the Black Panthers in 1969 is a case in point: the reporters closest to the Black Panthers could not dispute their public claim that an organized campaign of genocide was being waged against them without jeopardizing the special access they had to Panther spokesmen.

Moreover, since journalists generally lack the technical competence to evaluate evidence with any authority, they must also rely on the reports of authoritative institutions for their "facts." A reporter cannot establish the existence of an influenza epidemic, for instance, by conducting medical examinations himself; he must rely on the pronouncement of the Department of Health. (A journalist may of course become a doctor, but then his authority for reporting a fact rests on his scientific rather than journalistic credentials.) Whenever a journalist attempts to establish a factual proposition on his own authority, his conclusion must be open to question. For example, following the overthrow of the Allende government in Chile in 1973, *Newsweek* carried a dramatic report by a correspondent who claimed to have gained entrance to the Santiago morgue and personally examined the bodies of those killed after the coup.

By inspecting the hands of the corpses, and the nature of their wounds, the correspondent concluded that these were workers with callused hands who had been brutally executed. When the *Wall Street Journal* challenged these findings (on the basis of inconsistencies in the description of the morgue), the reporter acknowledged that he personally had spent only two minutes on the scene, and *Newsweek* fell back on an earlier unpublished report of a UN observer who claimed to have witnessed something similar in the Santiago morgue at some different time. While the dispute remained unsettled, the burden of proof was shifted from *Newsweek's* own reporter to an outside "authority."

Finally, journalists cannot even claim the modicum of authority granted to academic researchers because they cannot fulfill the requirement of always identifying their sources, let alone documenting their claims. Protecting (and concealing) the identity of their informants is a real concern for journalists, and one on which their livelihood might well depend, but it also distinguishes the journalistic from the academic product. Without identifiable sources the account cannot be reviewed or corroborated by others with specialized knowledge of the subject. Even the most egregious errors may thus remain uncorrected. For instance, in what purported to be an interview with John W. Dean III, the President's former counsel, *Newsweek* reported that Dean would reveal in his public testimony that some White House officials had planned to assassinate Panama's head of government, but that the plan was aborted at the last minute. This *Newsweek* "exclusive" was circulated to thousands of newspapers in an advance press release, and widely published. When it turned out that the story was untrue—Dean did not testify about any such assassination plot, and denied under oath that he had discussed any substantial aspects of his testimony with *Newsweek* reporters—*Newsweek* did not correct or explain the discrepancy. Presumably, Dean was not the source for the putative "Dean Interview," and the unidentified source had misled *Newsweek* on what Dean was planning to say in his public testimony. Since the error was that of an unidentified source, *Newsweek* did not feel obligated to correct it in future editions.

It is not necessary to belabor the point that gathering news is a very different enterprise from establishing truth, with different standards and objectives. Journalists readily admit that they are dependent on others for privileged information and the ascertainment of facts in a controversial issue (although some might argue that the sphere of measurable and non-controversial issues is larger than I suggest). Indeed, many of the most eminent journalists in America submitted affidavits in the Pentagon Papers case attesting that "leaks" and confidential sources are indispensable elements in the reporting of national news. And despite the more heroic public claims of the news media, daily journalism is largely concerned with finding and retaining profitable sources of prepackaged stories (whether it be the Weather Bureau, the Dow-Jones financial wire service, public-relations agencies, or a confidential source within the government). What is now called "investigative reporting" is merely the development of sources within the counter-elite or other dissidents in the government, while "stenographic reporting" refers to the development of sources among official spokesmen for the government. There is no difference in the basic method of reporting.

Even in the case of Watergate, which has become synonymous with "investigative reporting," it was the investigative agencies of the government and not the members of the press who assembled the evidence, which was then deliberately leaked to receptive reporters at the Washington *Post,* the Los Angeles *Times, Time,* and other journals. Within a week after the burglars were caught in Watergate in June 1972, FBI agents had identified the leaders of the break-in as employees of the Committee for the Reelection of the President (and former employees of the White House), traced the hundred-dollar bills found in their possession to funds contributed to President Nixon's reelection campaign, and interviewed one of the key conspirators, Alfred Baldwin, who in effect turned state's evidence, describing the wiretapping operation in great detail and revealing that the transcripts had been delivered directly to CRP headquarters.

This evidence, which was presented to the grand jury (and eventually in open court), was systematically leaked by investigative agents in the case. (Why members of the FBI and the Department of Justice had become dissidents is another question.) The crucial evidence which the FBI investigation did not turn up—such as the earlier burglary of Ellsberg's psychiatrist, the offers of executive clemency, the intervention with the CIA, the suborning of perjury, the cash payoffs made from campaign contributions, the "enemies list," and the 1970 subversion control plan—came out not through "investigative reporting," but only when one of the burglars, John McCord, revealed his role in the cover-up to Judge John Sirica and when John Dean virtually defected to the U.S. prosecutor and disclosed the White House "horror stories." Indeed, it was John Dean, not the enterprising reporters of the Washington press corps, who was the real author of most of the revelations that were at the heart of the present federal conspiracy indictments and the impeachment inquest. (And it was Ralph Nader, another non-journalist, who unearthed the contributions from the milk industry.) To be sure, by serving as conduits for the interested parties who wanted to release information about Watergate and other White House abuses of power, journalists played an extremely important role in the political process—but not as investigators or establishers of the truth.

The reliance on "leaks" or "authoritative" sources might not be an insoluble problem for journalism if reporters had some means of evaluating them in advance, and publishing only those portions which did not distort reality by being either untrue or out of context. Unfortunately, however, the inherent pressures of daily journalism severely reduce the possibility of verifying a leak or disclosure in advance of publication. Reporters can of course seek out more than one source on an issue, but there is no satisfactory way available, other than intuition, to choose among conflicting accounts. The democratic criterion of adding up confirming and disconfirming interviews, as if they were votes, produces no decisive result, as even total agreement might simply mean that a false account had been widely circulated, while total disagreement might mean that only the original source was privy to the truth about an event.

"Plausibility" is also an unsatisfactory criterion for evaluating leaks, since the liar is always capable of fashioning his account to fit the predispositions of the journalist to whom he is disclosing it, and thereby to make it appear plausible. Nor can a reporter simply give weight to the source that is most intimately involved with the issue, since those closest to a dispute might have the greatest interest in distorting or neglecting aspects of it, and might well be the least impartial. In certain instances, leaks, if publication were delayed, could be tested by the direction of unfolding events—for example, the advance disclosure of John Dean's testimony could have been refuted if *Newsweek* had delayed its story until Dean actually testified—but such a procedure would undercut the far more basic journalistic value of signaling the probable direction of events before they fully unfold. Given these circumstances, a journalist has little basis for choosing among conflicting sources. *The New York Times* thus carried two completely contradictory reports of the same insurrection in the Philippines in different sections of the same Sunday edition (February 17, 1974). The "News of the Week" section placed the casualties at 10,000 dead or missing, while the general news section refuted this higher figure and placed the total casualties at 276. Both accounts were based on sources within the Philippine government, and the editor of each section simply chose the account he preferred.

When journalists are presented with secret information about issues of great import, they become, in a very real sense, agents for the surreptitious source. Even if the disclosure is supported by authoritative documents, the journalist cannot know whether the information has been altered, edited, or selected out of context. Nor can he be certain what interest he is serving or what will be the eventual outcome of the leak.

Consider, for example, the disclosures by the columnist Jack Anderson of the minutes of a secret National Security Council meeting on the 1971 Indo-Pakistani war for which he was awarded the Pulitzer Prize for national reporting. Anderson claimed that the blunt orders by Dr. Henry Kissinger in these private meetings to "tilt" toward Pakistan contradicted Kissinger's public professions of neutrality; this claim received wide circulation, and sharply undermined Kissinger's credibility (although the *Wall Street Journal* demonstrated by printing the public statements to which Anderson referred that Kissinger was in fact consistent in both his private and public statements in expressing opposition to the Indian military incursion into East Pakistan). At the time it was generally presumed that the leak came from a dissident within the administration who favored India, or, at least, opposed the administration's policy in the subcontinent. Only two years afterward, as a by-product of the Watergate investigation, was some light cast on the source of the leak. A White House investigation identified Charles E. Radford, a Navy yeoman, who was working at the time as a stenographer, as the proximate source of the National Security Council minutes supplied to Anderson. But the investigation further revealed that Yeoman Radford was also copying and transmitting to members of the Joint Chiefs of Staff highly classified documents in a "surreptitious operation" apparently designed to keep them aware of Kissinger's (and the President's) negotiations. And Yeoman Radford has testified that he acted only on the express orders of the Joint Chiefs of Staff, and not on his own initiative, in passing documents. If this is indeed the case, it would appear that members of the Joint Chiefs of Staff authored the Anderson leak in order to undermine the authority of Henry Kissinger (who was involved in developing the détente with China and Russia at that time). In this case, Anderson was used as an instrument in a power struggle he probably was unaware of—and which might have had nothing to do with the Indo-Pakistani war he was reporting on.

The important question is not whether journalists are deviously manipulated by their sources, but whether they can exert any real control over disclosures wrenched from contexts to which they do not have access or with which they are unfamiliar. In most circumstances, the logic of daily journalism impels immediate publication which, though it might result in a prized "scoop," divorces the journalist from responsibility for the veracity or consequences of the disclosure. Jack Anderson was thus able to explain a blatantly false report he published about the arrest for drunken driving of Senator Thomas Eagleton, then the Vice-Presidential nominee of the Democratic party, by saying that if he had delayed publication to check the allegation he would have risked being scooped by competitors.

But even in rare cases in which newspapers allot time and manpower to study a leak, as *The New York Times* did in the case of the Pentagon Papers, the information still must be revised into a form and format which will maintain the interest of the readers (as well as the editors). Since the *Times* decided not to print the entire study of the Vietnam war—which ran to more than seven thousand pages and covered a twenty-five-year period—or even substantial parts of the narrative, which was complex and academic, sections of the material had to be reorganized and rewritten along a theme that would be comprehensible to its audience. The theme chosen was duplicity: the difference between what the leaders of America said about the Vietnam war in private and in public. The Pentagon study, however, was not written in line with this theme: it was an official Department of Defense analysis of decision-making and, more precisely, of how policy preferences crystal-

lized within the department. To convert this
bureaucratic study into a journalistic exposé of
duplicity required taking certain liberties with the
original history: outside material had to be added
and assertions from the actual study had to be
omitted. For example, to show that the Tonkin
Gulf resolution (by which in effect Congress authorized the escalation of the war, and which was
editorially endorsed at the time by most major
newspapers, including *The New York Times* and
the Washington *Post*) resulted from duplicity, the
Times had to omit the conclusion of the Pentagon
Papers that the Johnson administration had tried
to avoid the fatal clash in the Tonkin Gulf, and
had to add evidence of possible American provocations in Laos, which were not actually referred
to in the Pentagon Papers themselves.

Journalists, then, are caught in a dilemma.
They can either serve as faithful messengers for
some subterranean interest, or they can recast the
message into their own version of the story by
adding, deleting, or altering material. The first
alternative assures that the message will be accurately relayed to the intended audience, although
the message itself might be false or misleading.
The latter alternative, while lessening the source's
control over the message, increases the risk of
further distortion, since the journalist cannot be
aware of the full context and circumstances surrounding the disclosure. In neither case can journalists be certain of either the truth or the intended purpose of what they publish. Such a
dilemma cannot be remedied by superior newsmen or more intensive journalistic training. It

arises not out of defects in the practice of journalism, but out of the source-reporter relationship which is part and parcel of the structure of modern journalism.

To some degree, the tension in the dilemma could be alleviated if journalists gave up the pretense of being establishers of truth, recognized themselves as agents for others who desired to disclose information, and clearly labeled the circumstances and interests behind the information they reported so that it could be intelligently evaluated. By concealing the machinations and politics behind a leak, journalists suppress part of the truth surrounding the story. Thus the means by which the medical records of Senator Thomas Eagleton were acquired and passed on to the Knight newspapers (which won the 1973 Pulitzer Prize for disclosing information contained in these records) seem no less important than the senator's medical history itself, especially since copies of the presumably illegally obtained records were later found in the White House safe of John Ehrlichman. (In rifling through Larry O'Brien's personal files, the Watergate burglars were probably looking for material damaging to O'Brien and the Democrats; if they had succeeded, such material would no doubt have found its way into print by being leaked to "investigative journalists.") Similarly, the motives and circumstances behind the well-timed leaks to the press by elements in the Nixon administration which ultimately forced Justice Abe Fortas from the Supreme Court do not necessarily make a less important part of the story than any of the alleged improprieties committed by Fortas. And the leaks provided by senior executives in the FBI and other investigative agencies in an attempt to resist White House domination still remain the unreported part of the Watergate story.

Since journalists cannot expose these hidden aspects of a story without damaging the sources they are dependent on for information (and honors), they cannot realistically be expected to label the interest behind any disclosure. (Indeed, it is a practice among journalists to mislead their readers by explicitly denying as occasion arises that they received information from their real source.) Under these conditions, journalism can serve as an important institution for conveying and circulating information, and signaling changes in the direction of public policy and discourse, but it cannot serve as a credible investigator of the "hidden facts" or the elusive truths which determine them.

—*Commentary,* April 1974

DID THE PRESS UNCOVER WATERGATE?

A sustaining myth of journalism holds that every great government scandal is revealed through the work of enterprising reporters who by one means or another pierce the official veil of secrecy. The role that government institutions themselves play in exposing official misconduct and corruption therefore tends to be seriously neglected, if not wholly ignored, in the press. This view of journalistic revelation is propagated by the press even in cases where journalists have had palpably little to do with the discovery of corruption. Pulitzer Prizes were thus awarded this year to the *Wall Street Journal* for "revealing" the scandal which forced Vice-President Agnew to resign and to the Washington *Star/News* for "revealing" the campaign contribution that led to the indictments of former Cabinet officers Maurice Stans and John N. Mitchell (who were subsequently acquitted), although reporters at neither newspaper in actual fact had anything to do with uncovering the scandals. In the former case, the U.S. Attorney in Maryland had through dogged plea-bargaining and grants of immunity induced witnesses to implicate the Vice-President; and in the latter case, the Securities and Exchange Commission and a grand jury had conducted the investigation that unearthed the illegal contribution which led to the indictment of the Cabinet officers. In both instances, even without "leaks" to the newspapers, the scandals uncovered by government institutions would have come to the public's attention when the cases came to trial. Yet to perpetuate the myth that the members of the press were the prime movers in such great events as the conviction of a Vice-President and the indictment of two former Cabinet officers, the Pulitzer Prize committee simply chose the news stories nearest to these events and awarded them its honors.

The natural tendency of journalists to magnify the role of the press in great scandals is perhaps best illustrated by Carl Bernstein and Bob Woodward's autobiographical account of how they "revealed" the Watergate scandals.* The dust jacket and national advertisements, very much in the bravado spirit of the book itself, declare: "All America knows about Watergate.

All the President's Men (New York: Simon & Schuster, 1974).

Here, for the first time, is the story of how we know. . . . In what must be the most devastating political detective story of the century, the two young Washington *Post* reporters whose brilliant investigative journalism smashed the Watergate scandal wide open tell the whole behind-the-scenes drama the way it happened." In keeping with the mythic view of journalism, however, the book never describes the "behind-the-scenes" investigations which actually "smashed the Watergate scandal wide open"—namely, the investigations conducted by the FBI, the federal prosecutors, the grand jury, and the congressional committees. The work of almost all those institutions, which unearthed and developed all the actual evidence and disclosures of Watergate, is systematically ignored or minimized by Bernstein and Woodward. Instead, they simply focus on those parts of the prosecutors' case, the grand-jury investigation, and the FBI reports that were leaked to them.

The result is that no one interested in "how we know" about Watergate will find out from their book, or any of the other widely circulated mythopoeics about Watergate. Yet the non-journalistic version of how Watergate was uncovered is not exactly a secret—the government prosecutors (Earl Silbert, Seymour Glanzer, and Donald E. Campbell) are more than willing to give a documented account of the investigation to anyone who desires it. According to one of the prosecutors, however, "No one really wants to know." Thus the government's investigation of itself has become a missing link in the story of the Watergate scandal, and the actual role that journalists played remains ill understood.

After five burglars, including James McCord, who was an employee of the Committee for the Reelection of the President (CRP), were arrested in the headquarters of the Democratic National Committee in the Watergate complex on June 17, 1972, the FBI immediately located three important chains of evidence. First, within a week of the break-in, hundred-dollar bills found on the burglars were easily traced by their serial numbers through the Federal Reserve Bank at Atlanta to the Miami bank account of Bernard Barker, one of the burglars arrested in the Watergate. By June 22, the prosecutors had subpoenaed Barker's bank transactions, and had established that the hundred-dollar bills found in the burglary had originally come from contributions to the Committee for the Reelection of the President and specifically from checks deposited by Kenneth Dahlberg, a CRP regional finance chairman, and others. (Copies of these checks were leaked to Woodward and Bernstein by an investigator for the Florida state's attorney one month later, well after the grand jury was presented with this information—and they "revealed" it in the Washington *Post* on August 1.) And in early June, the treasurer of the Republican National Committee, Hugh W. Sloan, Jr., confirmed to the prosecutors that campaign contributions were given to G. Gordon Liddy, who by then was suspected of being the ringleader of the conspiracy.

Secondly, the FBI, in searching the premises

of the burglars, found, within twenty-four hours after their arrest, receipts, address books, and checks that linked E. Howard Hunt, White House consultant, to the conspiracy. (This information was leaked a few days later by the Washington police to Eugene Bachinski, a Washington *Post* reporter, and subsequently published in that newspaper.) The investigation into Hunt led the prosecutors to his secretary, Kathleen Chenow, who was flown back from England, and, in early July, confirmed that Hunt and Liddy were working on clandestine projects together, and had had telephone calls from Bernard Barker just before Barker was arrested in Watergate. (Months later, in September, defense attorneys who had been given the list of prosecution witnesses leaked Miss Chenow's name to Woodward and Bernstein, who then—after calling her—"revealed" this information to the public.) Thus, in early July, the prosecutors had presented evidence to the grand jury tying Hunt and Liddy to the burglars (as well as Liddy to the money).

The most important chain of evidence involved an eyewitness to the entire conspiracy. The day of the burglary, the FBI discovered a listening post at the Howard Johnson Motor Hotel, across the street from the Watergate, from which conspirators sent radio signals to the burglars inside Watergate (and received transmissions from electronic eavesdropping devices). By checking through the records of phone calls made from this listening post, the FBI easily located Alfred Baldwin, a former FBI agent, who had kept logs of wiretaps for the conspirators and acted as a lookout. By June 25, after the prosecutors offered Baldwin's attorney a deal by which Baldwin could escape prison, Baldwin agreed to cooperate with the government.

The main instrument for extracting information from reluctant witnesses like Baldwin was the prosecutors' skill in threatening, badgering, and negotiating. By July 5, less than three weeks after the burglars were apprehended, Baldwin sketched out the outlines of the conspiracy. He identified Hunt and Liddy as being at the scene and directing the burglary; he described prior break-in attempts, the installation of eavesdropping devices, the monitoring of logs of the eavesdropping, and the delivery of the fruits of the conspiracy to CRP. All this evidence was, of course, presented to the grand jury in mid-July. (Liddy's name was only mentioned in passing in the press on July 22, when he resigned from CRP, and it was not until the following October that Jack Nelson of the Los Angeles *Times* located and published an interview with Baldwin. To "top" the L.A. *Times*'s interview, Woodward and Bernstein erroneously reported that Baldwin had delivered the logs to three executives at CRP, Robert C. Odle, Jr., Glenn J. Sedam, Jr., and William E. Timmons. In fact, Baldwin delivered the logs to Liddy. In any case, the press was three months behind the prosecutors in disclosing Baldwin's vital account.) The prosecutors needed, however, a witness to corroborate Baldwin, since they realized that any single witness could be discredited by fierce cross-examination. The locating of Thomas J. Gregory, a student working as a minor spy for CRP, was critical for the prosecutors' case, since he was able to corroborate important elements in Baldwin's account. (Gregory's existence was never mentioned by the press until the trial.)

The prosecutors and the grand jury thus developed an airtight case against Liddy, Hunt and the five burglars well in advance of, and without any assistance from, Woodward, Bernstein or any other reporters. The case was presented to the grand jury and would certainly have been made public in the trial. At best, reporters, including Woodward and Bernstein, only leaked elements of the prosecutors' case to the public in advance of the trial.

By leaking fragments of the prosecutors' case, Woodward and Bernstein, as well as other journalists, did, of course, add fuel to the fire. But even here, they were not the only ones publicizing the case. Immediately after the arrest of the Watergate burglars and throughout the campaign, Senator George McGovern denounced Watergate in most of his speeches and suggested in no uncertain terms that the White House was behind the burglary. Indeed, his campaign staff hired Walter Sheridan, a former FBI agent on Robert Kennedy's staff, to help "get out" the story. On June 20, three days after the burglary, the Democratic National Committee commenced a civil suit against the Committee for the Reelection of the President that compelled the responsible officials in CRP to give statements under oath (Edward Bennett Williams represented both the Democratic National Committee and the Washington

Post). The General Accounting Office, an arm of Congress, and Common Cause, a quasi-public foundation, meanwhile forced Republican officials to disclose information about campaign contributions which indirectly added to the publicity about Watergate. Preliminary legal actions taken by the prosecutors (as well as the Florida state's attorney) also divulged important elements of the case. For example, in motions opposing bail for the defendants, the prosecutors disclosed in a brief filed June 23, 1972, that Mexican checks were deposited in Barker's account (although the press, until a month later, when the checks were literally handed to reporters, failed to pursue the "money tree" exposed in the bail motions). In short, even in publicizing Watergate, the press was only one among a number of institutions at work.

But what about Hunt and Liddy's superiors —Jeb Stuart Magruder and John Mitchell? The prosecutors were unable to develop a case against them, since as part of a cover-up, coordinated by the White House counsel John Dean, Magruder swore that he had given Liddy the contributions for a different purpose—to set up a system of informants—and this perjury was corroborated by Mitchell, by Herbert L. Porter, Magruder's assistant, and by Sally Harmony, one of Liddy's secretaries. But neither did Woodward and Bernstein nor any other reporters reveal the existence of the cover-up. The offers of executive clemency, the participation of Dean in the cover-up, the hush money, and the perjury did not emerge in the press in any serious form until after the trial of the Watergate burglars.

In the end, it was not because of the reporting of Woodward and Bernstein, but because of the pressures put on the conspirators by Judge John Sirica, the grand jury, and congressional committees that the cover-up was unraveled. After the Watergate conspirators were convicted, Judge Sirica made it abundantly clear that they could expect long prison sentences unless they cooperated with the investigation of the Senate Select Committee on Presidential Campaign Activities (the Ervin committee). One of the convicted burglars, James McCord, clearly not content with accepting such a prison sentence, wrote Sirica that perjury had been committed at the trial and the defendants had been induced by "higher-ups" to remain silent. Subsequently, McCord suggested that Magruder, Mitchell, and Dean all were involved in the planning of the burglary and cover-up.

While McCord's assertion turned out to be only hearsay evidence, obtained from Liddy, the grand jury was reconvened, the prosecutors subpoenaed Dean, and the Ervin committee began focusing on the roles of Dean and Magruder. To intensify the pressure on Dean, the prosecutors held long secret sessions with Liddy, and though Liddy steadfastly refused to discuss the case in these well-publicized sessions, the prosecutors intentionally promoted the story that Liddy was talking and implicating Dean and Magruder.

As President Nixon's transcripts confirm, the ruse succeeded: Dean believed that Liddy, who had attended meetings with him and Mitchell which eventually led to Watergate, was plea-bargaining with the prosecutors. Moreover, Dean believed that Magruder, who could also implicate him in both the planning of the burglary and the cover-up, was about to bargain with the prosecutors. And FBI Director L. Patrick Gray, in confirmation hearings before the Senate Judiciary Committee, was publicly suggesting that Dean had interfered in the investigation and lied to the FBI.

Dean realized that he could not testify before the Ervin committee or the grand jury without fatally perjuring himself. Since President Nixon was not able to offer him any safe way out of his predicament, and he feared that the President's assistants would eventually sacrifice him, Dean began negotiating with the prosecutors on March 31 for immunity, and bit by bit, they forced him to disclose the entire cover-up—including the payments of hush money, blackmail threats, offers of executive clemency, the suborning of perjury, etc. In April the prosecutors finally elicited evidence from Dean of the burglary of Daniel Ellsberg's psychiatrist's office and the other "horror stories." Four days after he heard Dean was bargaining with the prosecutors, Magruder also decided to plea-bargain, and corroborated Dean's story.

A final coherent picture of the planning and execution of Watergate, of the cover-up, and of the other "horror stories" was developed by the Ervin committee on television. The American public thus found out about Watergate in hundreds of hours of testimony elicited in plea-bargaining and negotiations for immunity by the prosecutors and then presented and tested in cross-examination by members of the Ervin committee.

What was the role of the press in all this? At best, during the unraveling of the cover-up, the press was able to leak the scheduled testimony a few days in advance of its appearance on television.

If Bernstein and Woodward did not in fact expose the Watergate conspiracy or the cover-up, what did they expose? The answer is that in late September they were diverted to the trail of Donald H. Segretti, a young lawyer who had been playing "dirty tricks" on various Democrats in the primaries. The quest for Segretti dominates both the largest section of their book (almost one-third) and most of their "exclusive" reports in the *Post* until the cover-up collapsed later that March. Unidentified sources within the government gave Bernstein and Woodward FBI "302" reports (which contain "raw"—i.e., unevaluated—interviews), phone-call records, and credit-card records, all of which elaborated Segretti's trail. Through the FBI reports and phone records, they located a number of persons whom Segretti had tried to recruit for his "dirty-tricks" campaign. The reporters assumed that this was all an integral part of Watergate, and wrote that "the Watergate bugging incident stemmed from a massive campaign of political spying and sabotage. . . . The activities, according to information in FBI and Department of Justice files, were aimed at all the major Democratic Presidential contenders." They further postulated that there were fifty other Segretti-type agents, all receiving information from Watergate-type bugging operations.

As it turned out, this was a detour, if not a

false trail. Segretti (who served a brief prison sentence for such "dirty tricks" as sending two hundred copies of a defamatory letter to Democrats) has not in fact been connected to the Watergate conspiracy at all. Almost all his work took place in the primaries *before* any of the Watergate break-ins in June 1972; he was hired by Dwight Chapin in the White House and paid by Herbert Kalmbach, a lawyer for President Nixon, whereas the Watergate group was working for the Committee for the Reelection of the President and received its funds from the finance committee. No evidence has been offered by anyone, including Woodward and Bernstein, that Segretti received any information from the Watergate group, and the putative fifty other Donald Segrettis have never been found, let alone linked to Watergate. In short, neither the prosecutors, the grand jury, nor the Watergate Committee has found any evidence to support the Bernstein–Woodward thesis that Watergate was part of the Segretti operation.

The behavior of the officials who steered Bernstein and Woodward onto this circuitous course makes in itself a revealing case study. Bernstein and Woodward identify their main source only under the titillating code-name of "Deep Throat," and indicate that "Deep Throat" confirmed their suspicion that Segretti and political spying were at the root of the Watergate conspiracy. But who was "Deep Throat" and what was his motivation for disclosing information to Woodward and Bernstein? The prosecutors at the Department of Justice now believe that the mysterious source was probably Mark W. Felt, Jr., who was then a deputy associate director of the FBI, because one statement the reporters attribute to "Deep Throat" could only have been made by Felt. (I personally suspect that in the best traditions of the New Journalism, "Deep Throat" is a composite character.) Whether or not the prosecutors are correct, it is clear that the arduous and time-consuming investigation by Woodward and Bernstein of Segretti was heavily based on FBI "302" reports, which must ultimately have been made available by someone in the FBI. The prosecutors suggest that there was a veritable revolt against the directorship of L. Patrick Gray, because he was "too liberal." Specifically, he was allowing agents to wear colored shirts, grow their hair long, and was even recruiting women. More important, he had publicly reprimanded an FBI executive. According to this theory, certain FBI executives released the "302" files, not to expose the Watergate conspiracy or drive President Nixon from office, but simply to demonstrate to the President that Gray could not control the FBI, and therefore would prove a severe embarrassment to his administration. In other words, the intention was to get rid of Gray.

Such a theory would be perfectly consistent with the information-disclosing activities of the source that led Bernstein and Woodward astray. Ironically, even on the wrong trail, the stalwart Bernstein and Woodward generated enough damaging publicity about "Watergate" to cause the White House to vilify them and the Washington *Post*, and thus elevate them to the status of journalistic martyr-heroes. If instead of chastising the press, President Nixon and his staff had correctly identified the "signals" from the FBI, and had replaced Gray with an FBI executive, things might have turned out differently. (But Gray, as it happened, had acquired damaging files from Hunt's safe, and could engage in his own information-releasing game, if threatened.)

Perhaps the most perplexing mystery in Bernstein and Woodward's book is why they fail to understand the role of the institutions and investigators who were supplying them and other reporters with leaks. This blind spot, endemic to journalists, proceeds from an unwillingness to see the complexity of bureaucratic in-fighting and of politics within the government itself. If the government is considered monolithic, journalists can report its activities, in simply comprehended and coherent terms, and show it to be an adversary out of touch with popular sentiments. On the other hand, if governmental activity is viewed as the product of diverse and competing agencies, all with different bases of power and interests, journalism becomes a much more difficult affair.

In any event, the fact remains that it was not the press which exposed Watergate; it was agencies of government itself. So long as journalists maintain their usual professional blind spot toward the inner conflicts and workings of the institutions of government, they will no doubt continue to speak of Watergate in terms of the David and Goliath myth, with Bernstein and Woodward as David and the government as Goliath.

THE PANTHERS
AND THE PRESS

In March 1970, William Shawn, the editor of *The New Yorker,* asked me to investigate reports about police killing officials of the Black Panther Party in various cities in the United States.

Between 4:40 and 4:52 A.M. on December 4, 1969, plainclothes police in Chicago, while executing a search warrant for illegal weapons, shot to death Fred Hampton, the twenty-one-year-old chairman of the Black Panther party of Illinois, and Mark Clark, a member of the party, in Hampton's apartment. Four days later, at about the same hour of the morning, the Los Angeles Special Weapons Tactics Team, dressed in black jumpsuits and black hats, moved on the Black Panther party headquarters in that city with another search warrant for illegal weapons, and in a heated gun battle, shot and seriously wounded three more Panthers. Commenting on these events, in San Francisco, Charles R. Garry, chief counsel and spokesman for the Black Panther party, whose membership at the time was estimated at between eight hundred and twelve hundred, declared to the press that Hampton and Clark were "in fact the twenty-seventh and twenty-eighth Panthers murdered by the police," and that the deaths and the raids were all "part and package of a national scheme by various agencies of the government to destroy and commit genocide upon members of the Black Panther Party."

Garry's assertion that twenty-eight members of the controversial black-militant group had been killed by the police was widely reported. On December 7 and December 9, 1969, *The New York Times* reported as an established fact, without giving any source for the figure or qualifying it in any way, that twenty-eight Panthers had been killed by police since January 1968. (These stories were disseminated throughout the country to over three hundred newspapers and news agencies that subscribe to the *Times* wire service.) On December 9, 1969, the Washington *Post* stated flatly, "A total of 28 Panthers have died in clashes with police since January 1, 1968." In a later article, the *Post* declared, "Between a dozen and 30 Panthers have been killed in these confrontations." (About two hundred newspapers subscribe to the *Post's* wire service.)

On the basis of what had been reported about the police killings and predawn raids, civil rights leaders expressed an understandable concern. Roy Innis, director of the Congress for Racial Equality, called for an immediate investigation of "the death of 28 Black Panther members killed in clashes with the police since January, 1968." Ralph Abernathy, who succeeded Martin Luther King, Jr., as the chairman of the Southern Christian Leadership Conference, attributed the death of Panther leaders to "a calculated design of genocide in this country." Julian Bond, a member of the Georgia state legislature, said, "The Black Panthers are being decimated by political assassination arranged by the federal police apparatus." And Whitney Young, executive director of the National Urban League, urgently requested the Attorney General to convene federal grand juries in those "jurisdictions where nearly 30 Panthers have been murdered by law-enforcement officials."

Garry's theory about "a national scheme . . . to destroy" the Black Panthers was also taken up by the press. Pointing to a "growing feeling (particularly in the black community)" that the "Federal Administration has had a hand in the recent wave of raids, arrests and shoot-outs," an article in the *Times* by John Kifner concluded that statements made by officials of the Nixon administration "appear to have at least contributed to a climate of opinion among local police . . . that a virtual open season has been declared on the Panthers." *Time* reported, on December 12, 1969, that "a series of gun battles between Panthers and police throughout the nation" amounted to a "lethal undeclared war," and concluded, "Whether or not there is a concerted police campaign, the ranks of Panther leadership have been decimated in the past two years." In the very next issue, *Time,* repeating Garry's claim that "28 Panthers have died in police gunfire," asked, "Specifically, are the raids against Panther offices part of a national design to destroy the Panther leadership?" The answer was more or less left open. That same week, *Newsweek* began a news report entitled "Too Late for the Panthers?" with the same question: "Is there some sort of government conspiracy afoot to exterminate the Black Panthers?" The article then proceeded to portray a "guerrilla war between the gun-toting Panthers and the police," in which the Panther "hierarchy around the country has been all but decimated over the past year," and concluded that "there is no doubt that the police around the nation have made the Panthers a prime target in the past two years," though it left it open as to whether or not the effort was systematic. A few weeks later, *Newsweek* reported that "the cop on the beat has been joined by Attorney General John Mitchell's Justice Department, which believes the Panthers to be a menace to national security and has accordingly escalated the drive against them" —a drive that "has taken a fearful toll of the Panthers." The Washington *Post,* noting in an editorial that the "carnage has been terrible" in the "urban guerrilla warfare" between Panthers and police, concluded that "recent events" had given "added currency" to the Panther charge that "there is a national campaign under way to eradicate them by any means, legal or extralegal." Picking up the theme in his syndicated column, Carl T. Rowan observed, "We have seen this nationally orchestrated police campaign to turn the guns on the Panthers and wipe them out," and referred to an "obvious conspiracy of police actions across the country that has produced the alleged killings of 28 Black Panthers." The *Nation,* in an editorial titled "Marked for Extinction," asserted, "It is becoming increasingly apparent that a campaign of repression and assassination is being carried out against the Black Panthers." Even a paper as cautious as the *Christian Science Monitor,* after a telephone interview with Garry, cited the Panther charge of "police murder" and "genocide" and expressed "a growing suspicion that something more than isolated local police action was involved."

Confusion about the alleged murders began to set in early, and on December 21, 1969, the *Times* reported that Garry had put the number of Panthers killed by the police at twelve, although it later returned to the figure of twenty-eight. While an Associated Press dispatch in the San Francisco *Examiner* on December 9 reported that twenty-seven Panthers had been killed by police in "Chicago, Denver, San Francisco, Detroit, and Indianapolis," the United Press International wire service, on December 12, sent out to its clients a list, provided by the Black Panther party, of twenty Panthers killed in "cold blood" by police in Los Angeles, Oakland, Seattle, San Diego, New Haven, and Chicago. (In the list itself, however, only sixteen deaths could actually be attributed to the police.) *Life,* in a single issue—that of February 6, 1970—presented three figures: Eldridge Cleaver, the minister of information of the Black

Panther Party, was quoted as saying that police "ambush" had led to "28 murders" of Panthers, but at another point the magazine declared, "So far, in the running guerrilla war of rooftop sniping, midnight ambush and mass shoot-outs that the Panthers and police have been waging in a number of cities . . . at least 19 Panthers are dead," adding, in parentheses, that "it is uncertain that more than a dozen have died of police bullets." While articles in the *New Republic, Ramparts,* and the *New Statesman* have, at various times, put the figure at twenty, an article in *Newsday* by Patrick Owens, who made a conscientious effort to check out Garry's claims, asserted that no more than ten Panthers had been killed by police. The executive director of the American Civil Liberties Union in Illinois declared, according to the Washington *Post,* that twenty-eight Panthers had died in clashes with police since January 1, 1968, while the Los Angeles branch of the same organization said that it was possible to document twelve cases in which Panthers had been killed in such encounters. In a column in the *Post* a few days earlier, Nicholas von Hoffman had written, "The Panthers alone claim that 28 of their top people have been murdered in the last couple of years, and there is no strong prima-facie reason to disbelieve them."

Even one victim of deliberate police murder would be too many, but if twenty-eight Panthers had been murdered by the police in two years, as Garry claimed and many publications reported, it might indeed represent a pattern of systematic destruction. The implications would be so dreadful that one would expect the figures to be checked out with the utmost scruple. Since the number of Panthers killed would seem to be an ascertainable fact, how can such widely differing figures be accounted for?

When A. M. Rosenthal, the managing editor of the *Times,* was asked about the discrepancies in his paper, he explained that the December 7 report, which stated, "Twenty-eight Black Panthers have been killed in run-ins with the police since January 1, 1968," was taken from a December 5 story by the same reporter, which said, "According to Charles Garry . . . [Hampton and Clark] were the 27th and 28th Black Panthers killed in clashes with the police since January of 1968," and which was itself based on a telephone conversation with Garry. In the December 7 story, the qualifying phrase "according to Charles Garry" had been deleted, Rosenthal said, because "the reporter probably felt the source was unimportant in the second story"—although Rosenthal, in discussing the matter, said that he personally felt that the reporter should not have turned an assertion by an interested party into a fact. The figure of twenty-eight had subsequently been reported as fact because the reporter "inadvertently referred to the first figure," and *this* had happened because "no flag was placed on the error." (Whitney Young's assertion that "nearly thirty Panthers have been murdered by law-enforcement officials" was based on the *Times,* according to his research assistant, and the *Times* was then able to report in a Sunday summary that the charge of a "national conspiracy" against the Panthers "has been echoed by more moderate civil-rights leaders.'')

Ben Bagdikian, the national editor of the Washington *Post,* also named Garry as the source for his newspaper's assertion that twenty-eight Panthers had been killed by police—though the only "specific documentation" on the subject was the U.P.I. bulletin of December 12. The U.P.I. bulletin, which went out to more than four thousand subscribing domestic newspapers and broadcasting stations, came from the news agency's San Francisco bureau, which, according to its manager, H. Jefferson Grigsby, obtained the list of "victims of cold-blooded murder by the police" from Panther sources. "There was no further dispatch modifying the December 12th story," Grigsby has noted. Garry's list apparently provided publications such as the *New Republic, Ramparts,* and the *New Statesman* with the "fact" that twenty Panthers had been killed by police (the figure was published without attribution), and *Ramparts,* in turn, furnished an organization called the Committee to Defend the Panthers— whose letterhead included the names of Norman Mailer, I. F. Stone, Ralph Abernathy, Pete Seeger, Ossie Davis, and Gloria Steinem—with what the committee called the "grim statistic" of twenty Panthers dead. Members of another committee concerned with the treatment that Black Panthers were receiving at the hands of the police—this one set up by former Supreme Court Justice Arthur Goldberg and Roy Wilkins, of the N.A.A.C.P.— were widely quoted as saying that "twenty-eight" and "nearly thirty" Panthers had been "murdered" by police, although Norman C. Amaker, the staff director of the committee, conceded that the list on which these statements were based "was compiled at the behest of their national attorney, Charles Garry."

And so it went. Although Garry was certainly an interested party in the controversy over what came to be called the war between the Panthers and the police, it is clear that his assertions were widely accepted at their face value, so even when modifications were made in the lists of casualties it was Garry's story that was being modified, and practically no independent checking was done. How, then, did Garry arrive at his figures? In September 1970, Garry explained to me that he chose the number twenty-eight when newsmen called him for a statement after the shooting of Hampton and Clark because that "seemed to be a safe number"; he added that he believed "the actual number of Panthers murdered by the police is many times that figure." When pressed for the names, however, Garry found he could "document" only "twenty police murders" of Panthers. The list of "twenty murders," which was sent to me from Garry's office, along with a warning that "the facts are not necessarily empirical," actually comprises only nineteen Panther deaths, and one of the nineteen deaths—that of Sidney Miller, in Seattle—is attributed by Garry not to police but to "a merchant who claimed he thought Miller was going to rob the store." In the coroner's records, the statement of the Seattle police is that "the deceased and an unknown person were robbing the Seven-Eleven store at 8856 35th Ave. S.W., and in the progress of the robbery the deceased was shot with a .38-caliber snub-nosed Smith & Wesson by the store owner, Donald F. Lannoye." Lannoye does not dispute the statement that he fired the fatal shot.

That leaves eighteen "documented" cases involving Black Panthers who Garry claims were murdered by police in pursuance of a conspiracy to "commit genocide upon" the Black Panthers. The way black people in general are treated by the police in our society has become a subject of increasing concern to many citizens, black and white, and, for a number of reasons—including the deaths of Hampton and Clark in Chicago—the idea of a deliberate police campaign against the Panthers may not seem far-fetched. But if there is to be an abatement of the fear and near-hysteria that seem to have developed around the question of the Panthers and the police, surely we must begin by getting the facts straight. For this reason, Garry's list of eighteen Panthers allegedly murdered by the police may be worth examining in some detail.

The Case of Alex Rackley

On May 21, 1969, John Mroczka, a twenty-three-year-old factory worker, stopped his motorcycle near a bridge on Route 147 outside of Middlefield, Connecticut, and while walking along the edge of a stream looking for trout saw a "set of legs" and "body" partly submerged. State police were called to the scene by Mroczka, and they recovered from the stream the body of a Negro male whose wrists were tied with gauze and whose neck was encircled by a noose fashioned from a wire coat hanger. An autopsy, conducted immediately afterward, indicated that the man had been severely burned on wide areas of the chest, arms, wrists, buttocks, thighs, and right shoulder and had also been beaten around the face, the groin, and the lumbar region with a hard object before he was shot in the head and chest. The victim, who was subsequently identified by his fingerprints as Alex Rackley, had died, a pathologist concluded, within the preceding twelve to twenty-four hours.

Just after midnight on May 22, New Haven police acted on a tip supplied by an informant who identified a Polaroid photograph of the corpse as a man who had been tortured with scalding water in an apartment that served as Panther headquarters in New Haven. Around 12:30 A.M., they raided the apartment and arrested Warren Kimbro, thirty-five, one of the leaders of the New Haven chapter of the Black Panther party, and five women members. Eventually, eight other Black Panthers, including Bobby Seale, the national chairman of the party, were arrested, and all of those arrested, except two who were remanded to a juvenile court, were charged with complicity, in varying degrees, in the kidnapping or torture or murder of Alex Rackley, a twenty-four-year-old member of the New York chapter of the Black Panther party.

Charles Garry immediately charged that "Rackley was killed by the police or by agents of some armed agency of the government." Holding that the murder victim was in "good standing" in the party, he further declared, as quoted in *News-*

week, "We have every reason to believe, and we intend to prove, when the time comes, that Rackley was murdered by police agents."

Even without proof, Garry's version of the events gained wide currency. The U.P.I.'s listing of Panthers alleged by a party spokesman to have been killed by the police cites "Alex Rackley" simply as " 'tortured and killed' by the police in New Haven, Conn., in May, 1969." At Yale, where a national May Day rally was held in the spring of 1970 to support the Panthers charged in the case, William Sloane Coffin, the Yale chaplain, described the trial of the accused Panthers as "Panther repression," and said, "All of us con-spired to bring on this tragedy—law-enforcement agencies by their illegal acts against the Panthers, and the rest of us by our immoral silence in front of these acts." At the same time, the president of Yale, Kingman Brewster, Jr., told striking stu-dents—who were demanding, among other things, the release of the Black Panthers awaiting trial for Rackley's murder—that he was "skepti-cal of the ability of black revolutionaries to achieve a fair trial anywhere in the United States," adding, "In large measure, the atmosphere has been created by police actions and prosecutions against the Panthers in many parts of the coun-try."

At this point, the three Black Panther officers who were specifically accused of taking Rackley to the stream near Middlefield, Connecticut, where his body was found had long since admitted their participation in the killing. George Sams, Jr., a twenty-three-year-old Panther who had once held

the rank of field marshal in the national Black
Panther party, pleaded guilty to second-degree
murder, which in Connecticut carries with it a
mandatory sentence of life imprisonment, and testified that in the early morning of May 21, 1969,
he and Warren Kimbro and Lonnie McLucas, using a car that McLucas had borrowed, took Rackley, bound and gagged, from Black Panther headquarters in New Haven to a deserted spot off
Route 147; there Kimbro, under Sams' direction,
shot Rackley in the head with a .45-caliber pistol,
and a few minutes later McLucas fired another
shot into the body. Sams testified that he was acting under orders from the "national" party personally given to him by Bobby Seale. Kimbro
pleaded guilty to second-degree murder in January 1970, and testified in open court that he fired
the first shot into the back of Rackley's head after
Sams said, "Now." Kimbro, however, refused to
implicate Seale in the crime, testifying that he
himself was asleep at the time Seale was said by
Sams to have visited the headquarters. McLucas,
twenty-three, a captain in the Black Panther party
and a founder of the Bridgeport chapter, gave the
same general account of the killing to New Haven
police detectives and FBI agents two days after he
was captured in Salt Lake City in June 1969. During his own trial, at which he pleaded not guilty
to the charge of conspiracy, McLucas testified that
he drove Rackley, bound and gagged, along with
Sams and Kimbro, from New Haven to Middlefield; after Kimbro had shot Rackley, McLucas
said, Sams ordered him, McLucas, "to make sure
he was dead." McLucas said he then fired a second

bullet into Rackley. McLucas, like Kimbro, has not implicated Seale, although he acknowledged under cross-examination that at the time of the killing he believed he was acting under orders from "national headquarters." (McLucas was found guilty of conspiracy to commit murder and sentenced to twelve to fifteen years in prison.)

The testimony of Sams, Kimbro, and McLucas was consistent with physical evidence that has not been contested in various legal proceedings having to do with the case—a .45-caliber pistol that the police found in Panther headquarters on the night of the raid ballistically matched the bullet and the bullet casing found at the scene of the murder, and fingerprints found on the car that McLucas borrowed that night matched those of Sams and Rackley—and also with the statements of other Panthers who were present in the apartment on the night of the killing. For example, Loretta Luckes, who had stood guard over Rackley while he was tied to a bed in the Panther headquarters for two days, described, in testimony during bail hearings, having helped to dress Rackley on the night of the murder while Sams and Kimbro stood over him with a pistol and rifle (because, one Panther said, "he might go crazy"); then, she said, "Lonnie [McLucas], Warren Kimbro and George Sams" went "out the door" with Rackley.

It may be that McLucas, Kimbro and Sams were acting under orders from Seale or the national Black Panther party, or it may be, as much of the testimony in the legal proceedings to date indicates, that some wildly irrational suspicions about Rackley turned an interrogation session into torture and murder. But the fact remains that Rackley was shot not by the police but by two officers of the Black Panther party, and since both have refused to implicate Seale, the suggestion that they might be "police agents" seems shaky at best. Perhaps Seale's trial for conspiracy now going on in New Haven will shed further light on the motive for the killing, but even at this stage of the legal proceedings it is difficult to take seriously Garry's inclusion of Rackley in his list of Panthers killed by the police.

The Case of Nathaniel Clark

Nathaniel Clark, Jr., a nineteen-year-old Black Panther, is listed by Garry as having been "killed by a police agent" and by the U.P.I., quoting the Black Panther party, as having been "killed by the police in Los Angeles." He was killed by his wife, who told investigating officers that she had shot her husband in self-defense with his revolver after he had, in her words, "shot up with heroin and beat me up." Because of her age, seventeen at the time, the case was remanded to a juvenile court, which adjudged the death to have resulted from involuntary manslaughter.

The Case of Arthur Morris

On March 13, 1968, while out on bail on a charge of conspiracy to commit murder, Arthur Glenn Morris (also known as Arthur Coltrale) was killed by a blast from a 12-gauge shotgun in a friend's back yard. According to the friend's wife, Mrs. Henry Daily, Morris and a companion, Donald Campbell, were in the back yard talking with her husband, who had taken his 12-gauge shotgun out there with him. She heard the men arguing, then heard a volley of shots. Rushing out, she found all three men fatally shot. Apparently, there had been a shoot-out, in which either Morris or Campbell had shot Daily with a .32-caliber automatic (the gun found at the scene) and he had shot both men with his shotgun. None survived to tell their stories.

The Case of John Huggins, Alprentice Carter, Sylvester Bell and John Savage

Of the fifteen remaining "homicides" on Garry's list, four Panthers—John Jerome Huggins, Jr., Alprentice (Bunchy) Carter, Sylvester Bell, and John Savage—were actually shot to death, according to both the Black Panther party and California authorities, by members of US, a rival black-militant organization, headed by Ron Karenga, with which the Panthers had once temporarily allied themselves in a lawsuit against the Los Angeles Police Department.

The dispute began at the University of California at Los Angeles in the fall of 1968, when Ron Karenga attempted to select the director of the Black Studies Program through the Community Advisory Board, of which he was a director. A number of Black Panthers, including Huggins and Carter, who were at that time enrolled in the black section of the "high-potential" program, vigorously opposed Karenga's attempt, despite the warning of a Karenga spokesman, who said, "This is not a decision that anybody is going to take out of our hands. . . . Anybody that is involved in this is going to have to come back to the community after dark." Leaders of US said that students who accepted Karenga's hand-picked director would be given "protection" against Panther reprisals. On January 17, 1969, some hundred and fifty members of the U.C.L.A. Black Students Union met in Campbell Hall on the U.C.L.A. campus to resolve the dispute over the directorship. Five members of the elite guard of US— known as Simbas, after the word for "lion" in Swahili—were present. Shortly after noon, in the student cafeteria, Huggins and Carter cornered a young Simba named Harold Jones, who had been accused of manhandling a female Panther earlier in the day, and began pummeling him. Suddenly another Simba, dressed in a dashiki, stepped up behind Huggins and fatally shot him in the back. A gun battle ensued, in which Carter was also shot to death before the Simbas fled.

Black Panthers who had been present at the meeting were reluctant to supply information at first, but they cooperated fully with the police and the prosecutor in identifying the assailants and finding witnesses after the prosecutor spoke to Garry, who, the prosecutor later reported, "instructed the local Panthers to help us in our investigation." Two of the Simbas, George Phillip Stiner and Larry Joseph Stiner, were brought to trial on charges of conspiracy to commit murder, were convicted, largely on the basis of the testimony of five Black Panther witnesses, and sentenced to life imprisonment. A third Simba, Donald Hawkins, was also convicted of conspiracy to commit murder, and was sentenced to an indefinite term in the detention program of the California Youth Authority. Two other Simbas indicted in connection with the same killings—Harold Jones and Claude Hubert, who are alleged to have done the actual shooting—are still fugitives. (Karenga, who was on a speaking tour of Eastern cities at the time of these shootings, was subsequently arrested and indicted in Los Angeles on torture charges in another case.)

In the aftermath of the gun battle in Campbell Hall, two more Black Panthers were killed by members of the US organization, according to both the Black Panther party and the police. "At about 3:30 P.M. on May 23rd in San Diego, California, Lt. John Savage, Black Panther Party, was murdered by a whitewashed Karangatang, a member of the US organization led by Ron (Everett) Karenga," the Black Panther newspaper reported, and it went on, "Mr. Karenga, better known as pork chop, is leading his culturalized pork chops in a futile attempt to destroy the Black Panther Party." The US member who shot Savage was eventually arraigned and pleaded guilty to a charge of manslaughter. A few weeks after Savage's death, another Panther, Sylvester Bell, who was selling the Black Panther newspaper in Otto Square in San Diego, was approached by three members of US, who, according to the Black Panther account of the incident, asked him, "Are you talking about us this week?" A fight broke out, during which Bell was joined by two fellow Panthers, and one of the three members of US drew a gun and fatally shot Bell. The San Diego police arrested three members of US and indicted them for murder. One was convicted of murder, and the two others were convicted as accessories. Since Garry himself and the Panthers assisted the authorities in the identification and prosecution of some of those involved in the killings, his subsequent inclusion of these four names in his list of Panthers murdered by the police appears to be disingenuous.

The Case of Franko Diggs

Franko Diggs, forty, who was a captain in the Black Panther party, was found fatally shot in the Watts section of Los Angeles on December 19, 1968. No witnesses to the shooting could be found, but the police identified the murder weapon from the bullets as a foreign-made 9-mm. automatic pistol. Almost a year later, when the Los Angeles police crime laboratory was doing routine ballistics tests on eighteen weapons seized in a raid on Black Panther headquarters early in 1969, it was found that one of the confiscated Panther automatics ballistically matched the bullet that had killed Diggs. The chain of ownership could not be established, however, so the owner at the time Diggs was shot could not be identified. According to the police, the crime remains unsolved, but Garry, almost a year after Diggs' death, added his name to the list of Black Panthers killed by police. A doubtful matter at best.

*   *   *

The ten remaining Black Panthers on Garry's list
were in fact killed by the police—five in 1968 and
five in 1969. Whether these deaths were deliberate
murders carried out as part of what Garry called
a "national scheme" to wipe out the Panthers depends, of course, on the circumstances under
which each of the deaths occurred.

The Case of Larry Roberson

In summarizing the deaths of various Black Panthers, the *Times* quoted "sources in Chicago" as
saying that Larry Roberson "died in jail after being wounded in [a] shoot-out during [a] police
raid"—a statement suggesting that he was shot
during a planned police action against a Panther
office.

The picture of what happened that can be
pieced together from police records, independent
witnesses and even the Black Panther newspaper
is very different. At 2:01 A.M. on July 16, 1969, the
Chicago police received a "citizen's complaint"
that a fruit stand had been burglarized at 610
California Street, in the West Side ghetto. A radio
dispatcher routinely recorded this information on
a computer card used for statistical analysis of
complaints and crime patterns, and dispatched the
patrol car that his electronic map indicated was
nearest to the scene—Car No. 1124, manned by
Officers Kenneth Gorles and Daniel Sampila. According to Sampila's subsequent report, the officers arrived at the fruit stand at about 2:05 A.M.
and were met by Mr. and Mrs. Burman Jenkins,

friends of its owner, who pointed out a hole in the door of the stand. The two policemen, led by Mr. and Mrs. Jenkins, then followed a trail of apples and oranges to a passageway, where they found two empty fruit baskets. While the police were flashing a searchlight around, the group encountered Larry Roberson, twenty-one, and Grady Moore, twenty-eight, who identified themselves as "community leaders," and were told by Sampila to "mind their own business." The group, followed by Roberson and Moore, then returned to the fruit stand, where they were met by the Reverend Edmond Jones, who owned the fruit stand, and another of his friends, the Reverend Clarence Edward Stowers, who was the pastor at the nearby Mars Hill Missionary Baptist Church. A few minutes later, the two policemen and Jenkins were shot. In a statement Stowers made later, he described what happened this way:

Reverend Jones, Mr. Jenkins, myself, and the two officers were standing there talking about boarding up the door. Two men walked up and started looking in the hole in the door and asking what had happened. The officers told them that everything was taken care of and they should leave. One of the men had his hand in his pocket, and the officer shined his light on the man. The man asked him why was he shining the light on him and don't be doing that. Then the shooting started. The officers had their guns in their holsters so it must have been the men that were shooting. One of the officers fell down and the other one got hit in the shoulder. I remember it was only one of the two men that was shooting. He turned and ran up the alley. I don't know where the other one went to. Well, anyway the policeman that had fallen to the ground started chasing the man up the alley and lots of shots were fired.

Jones gave a similar account of the incident:

The policeman and Mr. Jenkins told Reverend Stowers and me that they hadn't found anything and that I could nail a board or something across the door. While we were talking two guys came across the playlot from Flournoy Street and started asking a lot of questions. The tall guy [Moore] went and looked in the door and the policeman told them that they had everything under control and for them to go about their business. The tall guy started mouthing at the policeman and then the other guy [Roberson] came up and hollered, "What's happening?" And he started shooting. One of the policemen [Sampila] fell to the ground right at my feet and the two guys started running. The policeman that had fallen by me got up and started chasing the man that was shooting at us. They ran down the alley and I heard more shots.

Mr. and Mrs. Jenkins agreed with this account, Mr. Jenkins adding:

One man shouted something and started shooting . . . after the first shot one officer fell to his knees, the second shot hit officer Gorles, and the third shot hit me.

Roberson, pursued through the alley, was shot in the ankle, in the thigh, and in the abdomen by Sampila before he surrendered. According to the Chicago crime laboratory, the bullets that struck Gorles (in the left shoulder and collarbone), Sampila (in the head), and Jenkins (in the right side) all came from a .38-caliber snub-nosed Smith & Wesson taken from Roberson. This turned out to be a stolen weapon. Roberson was arrested on charges of attempted murder and was admitted to the Cermak Memorial Hospital, where he underwent surgery. Seven weeks later, he contracted jaundice and died in the Cook County Hospital.

A somewhat different version of the incident was provided by the Black Panther newspaper, which reported, in August:

On July 17, 1969, two brothers in the Illinois chapter of the Black Panther Party were returning to their community after finishing a day of revolutionary work for the people's Party. On this particular night they noticed the pigs had nine brothers on the wall next to a storefront, harassing them. Five of the brothers were in ages ranging from 50–62 years old. The pigs claimed they were answering a burglary in process call. Can you imagine men 50–62 years old burglarizing a store in their own community? Well, after investigating the matter and coming to the conclusion that this was just another racist act of harassment committed by the pigs on the people, Larry Roberson and Grady Moore walked over to the scene where the majority of the people had gone and asked an officer what was going on. The pig then demagogically replied "This is none of your damn business." Br. Larry then stated "I am a member of this community and even by your laws I have the right to know what's going on." The crazy pig then said "Smart bastard, you're under arrest for disorderly conduct." The people of the community immediately got between Larry and the pigs, and the pig drew his gun and ordered them aside while his pig partner radioed for help. Larry then (with the instructions from the people) was told to go home because the people hadn't seen him do anything, so he and Grady started away and the pig deliberately shot Larry in the leg. Grady grabbed Larry to help him to try to escape with his life. This whole area was sealed off with crazy, drunk, inhuman pigs. Larry was then cornered in an alley, unarmed and wounded. As the pig approached him, he oinked "I'll teach you and your partner how to interfere with pig matters." He then aimed at Larry's head. It was true that Larry was unarmed, but being a Panther and a stone revolutionary, he had educated the true power—the people. As the pig was ready to squeeze the trigger, the power of the people was demonstrated. A voice quoted Huey: "You racist pigs must withdraw immediately from the black community and cease this wanton murder and brutality of black people or face the wrath of the armed people." Then, the shots from the people rang out from everywhere for about 30 seconds; then it ceased. One pig shot in the head and one pig shot in the shoulder. Larry and Grady then started to make it when more pigs arrived. Larry and Grady turned and raised their hands. The pig that was shot in the shoulder raised his gun and shot Brother Larry in the stomach, thigh and leg trying to kill him. Grady evidently escaped death when the people in the community came out to witness the action. . . . Larry Roberson is proven to be a true revolutionary not by words but by deeds. He has shown his love for the people. He put his life on the line and in return the people released some revolutionary power.

The statements that Roberson was unarmed and that the "people" did the shooting were contradicted by a subsequent report in the Black Panther newspaper, which said that "determined to defend himself even after being shot, Larry managed to get his gun out and wound two of the attacking maniacs." But the Panther version and the police version actually agree in a number of significant respects: the encounter was accidental; the Panthers approached the police rather than the other way around; and two police officers were shot *before* Roberson was seriously wounded in the abdomen.

The Case of Bobby Hutton

According to *Life,* Bobby Hutton, the seventeen-year-old minister of finance of the Black Panther party, was killed and Eldridge Cleaver was wounded in an "Oakland police ambush" in 1968. The *Times* quoted Garry as attributing Hutton's death to a "police ambush."

Shortly after 9 P.M. on April 6, 1968, Officers Nolan R. Darnell and Richard R. Jensen, while on routine patrol in the area of Oakland, California, that is predominantly inhabited by blacks, stopped their patrol car on Union Street next to a parked 1954 Ford when they caught a glimpse of a man crouching at the curb side of the car. In their report, they said that they suspected he might be trying to steal it. Moments later, while investigating the situation, both officers were hit by bullets fired from behind them. Afterward, forty-nine bullet holes were found in the police car, the rear window had "two large areas shot inward," and the side windows and the open door, next to which Darnell was standing at the time, had also been hit numerous times. According to medical reports prepared by Dr. William Mills, Jr., of Samuel Merritt Hospital, Darnell was wounded in the "upper right back." Jensen, apparently hit by a blast from a 12-gauge shotgun, suffered multiple wounds in the "lower right back," in the "right arm," and in the "right ankle and foot." According to Darnell, a number of men armed with shotguns and rifles ran from cars parked behind and ahead of the 1954 Ford, some of them through an alley into the block across the street, while Darnell urgently called for help on the police radio.

An account of the incident in the Black Panther newspaper said, "Several Panthers in cars in West Oakland on Saturday night, April 6th, were approached by two pigs and menaced with guns. When the Panthers tried to defend themselves, shooting began, and the Panthers ran into a nearby house. . . . Two pigs were wounded slightly." Four Black Panthers gave statements to the police in which they said that they had been patrolling the neighborhood with guns, in three cars, "to protect Negroes against police brutality," and had just parked their cars on Union Street in order to stow their weapons in a nearby house when the patrol car pulled up, but the four disclaimed any knowledge of how the shooting began. Cleaver later said in an interview that was published in the San Francisco *Chronicle,* "I don't know how those cops got shot. There were so many bullets whizzing around maybe they shot themselves."

In any event, after the two policemen were shot, police from other parts of West Oakland and even from nearby Emeryville, responding to the radio alarm, surrounded a building on Twenty-eighth Street that the Panthers had entered, and there ensued a ninety-minute gun battle, in which a third policeman was wounded. Finally, after an exploding tear-gas canister had set fire to the building, two Panthers emerged: Cleaver, naked, and wounded by a tear-gas shell, and Hutton, fully clothed. According to police witnesses, Hutton suddenly bolted down Twenty-eighth Street, whereupon at least half a dozen policemen opened fire, fatally wounding him. Cleaver, in the *Chronicle* interview, gave a different version of the shooting of Hutton. He admitted that Hutton had fired some shots at the police, but said that he himself "took Bobby's gun and threw it out"—out the window, that is—and that they both came out unarmed. "The cops told us to get up and start running for the squad car," Cleaver continued. "Bobby started running—he ran about ten yards—and they started shooting him." The grand jury, after hearing thirty-five witnesses, concluded that the police had "acted lawfully," shooting Hutton in the belief he was trying to escape.

Eight other Panthers, including Cleaver, who were allegedly involved in the shooting of the policemen were arrested that night and then were released on bail. Two of the eight were subsequently convicted of assault with deadly weapons; one was released to a juvenile court; one was tried and convicted for an unrelated armed robbery and sent to state prison; one, Cleaver, jumped bail and fled the country; two others, with the juvenile, are now on trial in Oakland; and other cases are still pending.

The Cases of Steven Bartholomew, Robert Lawrence, and Thomas Lewis

At about 4:45 P.M. on August 5, 1968, in a predominantly Negro section of Los Angeles, three Black Panthers were fatally shot and two policemen were wounded, one critically, in a shoot-out at Ham's Mobil Service Station.

Fifteen minutes earlier, Police Officers Rudy Limas and Norman J. Roberge were on a routine patrol when, according to their reports, they saw a black 1955 Ford with four men in it start up a private driveway, stop suddenly, then back down the driveway. Finding the movements suspicious, the policemen began following the Ford, whose occupants, Limas noted, kept "looking back." Limas then called the police communications center on the patrol car's radio and gave the Ford's license number, to ascertain whether it had been reported stolen. Before a reply could be received, the Ford pulled into Ham's service station and stopped by a gas pump. The police car stopped a few feet behind it, and Roberge, according to his statement, asked the driver of the Ford for his license. The driver, Roberge reported, "replied that he didn't have any driver's license," whereupon Roberge "instructed the driver to go back to the police car and place his hands on top of the police car." Roberge then ordered the three other suspects out of the Ford and over to the police car. "At this time," Roberge stated, "the suspects were standing in a row facing the police vehicle"—between the two police officers.

Limas gave the following description of what happened next: "Suddenly the guy in front of me, who I think was wearing a yellow shirt and dark pants, spun around and pointed a gun at me, and the others moved at the same time. The guy in the yellow shirt said, 'O.K., m——f——' and then he shot me." According to medical reports and testimony, Limas was shot in the abdomen and the thigh, with a bullet lodging in the hip. Roberge

stated, "As I walked toward the police vehicle, I
saw my partner, Officer Limas, standing to the left
rear of the police vehicle on the other side of the
group, facing me. Suddenly I heard some shots
and I was knocked to the ground." According to
the medical evidence, Roberge was shot in both
legs. In the gun battle that followed, Limas fatally
shot "the guy in the yellow shirt" and a second
suspect, who was "trying to load a 9-mm. pistol,"
and Roberge "emptied" his gun at a third suspect.
The fourth man who had been in the car fled on
foot.

There were two independent witnesses to the
shooting—the service-station attendants, Shoji
Katayama and Eugene Oba. Katayama, who explained that he was "standing by the pumps
. . . a few feet east of the Ford," also stated in a
deposition:

A black (4-door) Ford pulled into the station, pursued by a police car. . . . There were 4 Negroes in the
Ford. The driver and front passenger both got out and
opened the hood of the car. The two officers immediately got out and ordered all four to the police car with
their hands leaning on it. The driver of the Ford looked
like to me he hesitated a while and was smoking a
cigarette. As the driver with the cigarette came to the
car, the Mexican officer [Limas] ordered him not to put
out the cigarette [near the pumps], and at that point [I]
heard a couple of shots and I looked up and saw the
Mexican officer on the ground and the male Negro with
the khaki shirt (Army type) with the gun in his
hand. . . .

The other attendant, Oba, had been returning
to the office when the shooting began. He gave a

similar account of the incident, adding only that after the first round of shots he "saw the Caucasian officer [Roberge] shooting at the Negro men."

When the shooting stopped, a few minutes later, three men were dead or dying—Thomas Melvin Lewis, eighteen, "the guy in the yellow shirt"; Robert A. Lawrence, twenty-two; and Steven Kenneth Bartholomew, twenty-one. The Black Panther party stated that they were all Black Panthers. The fourth suspect, who was subsequently identified by his palm prints on the police car as Anthony Reno Bartholomew, the nineteen-year-old brother of Steven, later surrendered voluntarily to a judge, and was arraigned on two counts of assault with intent to commit murder. Anthony Bartholomew's lawyer, Gary Bellow, a well-known civil rights attorney who has handled a number of Black Panther cases in Los Angeles, noted in a memorandum filed with the court, "There is no dispute that the police officers, Norman Roberge and Rudy Limas, were criminally assaulted on August 5, 1968," but went on to argue that his client had not in fact taken part in the gun battle. Anthony Bartholomew was found not guilty.

The Case of Walter Pope

Walter Touré Pope, whom Garry listed simply as "killed by Metro Squad," was shot to death by Officer Alvin D. Moen in a vacant lot across from the Jack-in-the-Box drive-in restaurant in Los Angeles on October 18, 1969.

On that night, Officer Moen and his partner,

Officer Don Mandella, were assigned to a robbery stakeout of the Jack-in-the-Box, which had been robbed fourteen times in the previous seven months. Sitting in an unmarked car, which they had parked in a lot across the street from the restaurant, the officers began their watch shortly after dark. At about 10:45 P.M., Moen later testified, he heard a noise behind him and "turned around and saw a man standing with what appeared to be a burp gun . . . pointed in my direction." Shouting, "Look out!" to Mandella, Moen, who was sitting behind the wheel, drew his service revolver. Then, according to his testimony, the man fired a shot, and Moen returned the fire. Suddenly, from the other side of the car, there came what Moen called "another loud explosion," which he identified as a shotgun blast. According to medical reports, Moen was hit in the back of the right shoulder and the back of the left hand by shotgun pellets. Although he was badly wounded, he managed to get out of the car, empty his revolver at the man with the burp gun, and then run to the restaurant for help. Mandella gave a similar account, testifying that after his partner shouted, "Look out!" two shotgun blasts were fired into the car from the passenger side as the man with the burp gun approached from the opposite side. Mandella then turned and fired three shots at the assailant with the shotgun, who fled. Picking up the microphone, he urgently requested assistance, saying that he and Moen had been "ambushed." When other policemen arrived, they found Walter Touré Pope, twenty, who was subsequently identified by the Black Panthers as their "distribution manager" for Los Angeles, shot to death beside the police car. He had a two-inch revolver tucked in his belt, and there was a .30-caliber carbine, or "burp gun," lying under his left arm. A sawed-off shotgun, both barrels of which had been fired, was found a few feet behind the police car. (Another Black Panther, Bruce Darryl Richards, eighteen, was arrested later that night at the U.C.L.A. Medical Center, where he was being treated for bullet wounds, and was charged with taking part in the assault. He pleaded not guilty but was subsequently convicted on two counts of assault with intent to commit murder.)

The only witnesses to the shooting were those who took part in it, and thus the question of who shot first may be open to doubt—although the medical evidence that Moen was hit by a shotgun blast in the back would seem to suggest that the police were approached from behind.

The Case of Welton Armstead

In Seattle, at about 4:10 P.M. on October 5, 1968, Welton Armstead, seventeen, was shot to death by a police officer in front of a house at 1706 Melrose Avenue. A few minutes earlier, Officers Erling Buttendahl and Charles Marshall, on a routine patrol, had received a radio message directing them to help Car No. 128 in a stolen-auto case at 1700 Melrose Avenue. When they arrived on the scene, they helped the policemen in Car No. 128 apprehend two of three suspects they had been pursuing. According to Buttendahl, while he was searching for the third suspect he came around the side of a house and was confronted by a man, later identified as Armstead, a Black Panther, standing next to the garage, "holding a rifle with both hands and pointing it" at him. According to the coroner's report, the armed man was asked four times to "drop the rifle" but refused to do so; instead, with one hand he grabbed the barrel of Buttendahl's revolver, raising his rifle with the other, whereupon, Buttendahl says, he himself fired, hitting Armstead in the midsection. An inquest jury, after hearing fourteen witnesses and considering the medical evidence, ruled the shooting "justifiable homicide." Garry does not dispute the fact that Armstead faced Buttendahl with a rifle.

The Case of Spurgeon Winters

On November 13, 1969, Spurgeon (Jake) Winters was shot to death by police on Martin Luther King Drive on Chicago's South Side. Earlier that evening, James Caldwell, a black prison guard at the Cook County Jail, had told his wife, Ruby, that he needed some money to rent a room for the night, because "some guys are looking for me and they want to kill me." The night before, he had been in a brawl outside the Rumpus Room tavern with Lawrence (Lance) Bell, a Black Panther, and had taken Bell's gun from him, and he feared reprisal from Bell and his friends. A few hours after Caldwell parted from his wife, someone entered the building where they lived and began pounding on apartment doors and calling Caldwell's name. Looking out a front window after the pounding had stopped, Mrs. Caldwell saw what she subsequently described as "four or five men leaving my building . . . one of them . . . carrying a long gun." She then went across a connecting porch to her sister-in-law's apartment in an adjacent building, where she asked a friend, Lee Wesley, for advice. Wesley said, she later told police investigators, that she "didn't have any choice but to call the police," because "if James came back they would kill him." Wesley himself then called the police.

At 2:49 A.M., a police dispatcher received a report that there were "men on the street with shotguns," and at 2:53 A.M., according to the police computer cards and radio tapes, the dispatcher ordered the nearest patrol car, No. 226, manned by Officers John Gilhooly and Michael Brady, to 324 East Fifty-eighth Street, the sister-in-law's apartment. Three other policemen joined them at the sister-in-law's apartment, which was at the rear of the building, and all five were then taken, across the connecting porch, to Mrs. Caldwell's apartment, where, from the front window, Mrs. Caldwell and Wesley pointed out to them three men lurking in an abandoned building across the street. Leaving by the front door, the policemen crossed over to the vacant building, and Gilhooly started to go in through a gangway. Mrs. Caldwell stated, "We could hear the policeman by the gangway shouting 'Halt!' about three times. Then we heard a loud shot, and it sounded louder than a pistol shot. Then we heard some more shots. . . . Then we saw the policeman come out of the gangway. He was saying 'Oh! Oh!' and he was holding his face." Gilhooly was fatally wounded, a shotgun blast having severed his carotid artery and his jugular vein; Brady had suffered minor lacerations of the forehead from the ricochet of a shotgun blast.

Mrs. Caldwell called the police to report that a policeman had been shot. At 3:04 A.M., the dispatcher put out an emergency call: "Police officer needs help." Twenty-one patrol cars in the area immediately responded.

Another policeman was wounded almost immediately by shotgun blasts, according to police reports, and one police car was "demolished" by carbine fire. One of the gunmen, who was allegedly carrying a carbine, and who was later identified as Bell, was shot in cross fire, and was captured. Meanwhile, three policemen had chased another man, carrying a shotgun, down an alleyway paralleling Martin Luther King Drive. He wounded all three and, taking refuge under the porch of a house on the Drive, shot another policeman, Frank Rappaport, in the chest and head, killing him, and wounded another. Two policemen, including the one who had just been wounded, emptied their revolvers at him, fatally wounding him. The dead gunman was later identified as Spurgeon (Jake) Winters. In all, two policemen were killed and seven wounded or hurt. Bell was indicted by a grand jury for murder. The case is pending.

The Black Panther version of the incident was similar to the police version in a number of respects. A "special news bulletin" put out by the Illinois chapter stated:

On November 13, 1969, Jake Winters stood face to face and toe to toe, his shotgun in his hand, with Pig Daley's murderous task force. He defined political power by blowing away racist pig Frank Rappaport and racist pig John Gilhooly and retired 8 other reactionary racist pigs before he was shot down.

The Black Panther newspaper reported the shootings this way:

Spurgeon (Jake) Winters, 19, member of the Illinois chapter of the Black Panther party, paid the most that one can pay towards the liberation of oppressed people—his life. At 3:30 A.M., November 13, Jake was murdered in a shoot-out in Chicago where three pigs were killed and seven were wounded. The shoot-out was precipitated by an ambush made by the Standing Army of Chicago (Chicago Police Department) on an abandoned building at 5801 S. Calumet. Arriving on the scene with the armaments and men (more than 1,000 policemen equipped with .12-gauge shotguns, M-1 carbines, .357 magnums, billy clubs, mace, tear gas, paddy wagons, helicopters, and canine units) for domestic warfare against the people in the Black colony, these fanatical pigs started their attack by opening fire on the brother in the building. Party comrade, Lance Bell, 20, was wounded by the pigs as they shot wildly in that area. . . . Jake defended himself as any person should do. In essence, he had no choice; it was kill or be killed.

There may be some room for doubt whether the police were in fact mounting an "ambush," as the Panthers claim, or were simply responding to a call originally issued in the belief that James Caldwell's life was in danger, but the Panthers and the police agree that after the police arrived at least eight policemen were shot before Winters was shot.

The Case of Fred Hampton and Mark Clark

The final case on Garry's list is certainly the most important one, since it is the one that prompted Garry to speak of a pattern of "genocide." It involves the fatal shooting of Fred Hampton and Mark Clark by policemen attached to the State's Attorney's office in Chicago on December 4, 1969. While there may be varying degrees of uncertainty about some of the other deaths on Garry's list, these two unquestionably resulted from a deliberately planned raid on a Black Panther headquarters.

On December 3, Sergeant Daniel Groth, a twelve-year veteran of the Chicago Police Department who had been assigned to the State's Attorney's Special Prosecutions Unit, told Assistant State's Attorney Richard S. Jalovec, who was in charge of the unit, that he had received information from a "confidential informer" that a cache of illegal weapons, including sawed-off shotguns, and also riot guns stolen from the Chicago police, was stored in a Black Panther apartment at 2337 West Monroe Street. Having received information from the Federal Bureau of Investigation just the day before that the Panthers had recently moved weapons to that address, Jalovec immediately ordered Groth to plan a raid on the Panther apartment, and Jalovec prepared a search-warrant complaint. Circuit Judge Robert Collins signed a warrant later that afternoon.

Groth and thirteen other policemen assigned to the Special Prosecutions Unit assembled at the State's Attorney's office at four the next morning.

They were heavily armed: five had shotguns, one had a Thompson submachine gun, and one— James Davis, one of the five black members of the raiding party—carried with him a .30-caliber carbine of his own. The raid was planned for dawn, to achieve the maximum surprise and minimum potential for neighborhood interference, according to Groth's later testimony.

The raiding party arrived at the West Monroe Street apartment in three cars and an unmarked panel truck, and Groth, Davis and three of the other members proceeded to the front door of the apartment, which was on the first floor; six members went around to the back door; and the three remaining members were stationed at the front of the building. At approximately 4:40 A.M., Groth pounded on the apartment door with his revolver butt. There are markedly different versions of what happened next.

In the police version, which was published in the Chicago *Tribune,* Groth shouted, "This is the police! I have a warrant to search the premises!" and then, after a delay, had Davis kick the door open. The two men entered a small hallway, where they were faced with another closed door. Suddenly, the police said, a shotgun blast from inside was fired through this door and "narrowly missed the two policemen." Davis then plunged through the inner door into a darkened living room, with Groth behind him, as a "second round went right past" him. Groth fired two shots at a woman who, he said, had fired the second shotgun blast, while Davis, after also firing at the woman and wounding her, turned and shot to death a man sitting behind him with a shotgun, who was later identified as Mark Clark. Moments later, three of the members of the raiding party who had gone around to the back broke in through the kitchen door of the apartment. Despite a number of calls for a cease-fire from Groth, the Panthers kept firing shotgun blasts, according to the police version of the events, and a "fierce fire fight" ensued, in which Hampton was killed and four other Panthers and one policeman were wounded.

In the Panther version, as it was reported in the Washington *Post,* the police burst into the apartment almost simultaneously through the front and rear entrances, without first identifying themselves, and although no Panthers fired any shots whatever, the police opened fire, also without warning. A Black Panther spokesman was reported in the *Post* to have said that Mark Clark was fatally wounded as he attempted to dodge police submachinegun fire, and others were wounded. Meanwhile, according to the spokesman, the police entering from the rear went immediately to Hampton's bedroom and fired into it, and Davis then went into the bedroom and fired more shots at Hampton. In *Chicago Today,* the Black Panther spokesman added that "Hampton was murdered in bed while he slept" by a policeman who "must have come in the back door and murdered him with a silencer." A few days later, a private autopsy, performed at the request of Hampton's family, concluded that hours before Hampton was shot to death he had been heavily drugged with Seconal, a barbiturate, which the spokesman deduced had been administered by a "pig agent" before the raid. The independent autopsy also concluded that the bullet that killed Hampton was missing, for the Panthers' pathologist found an entrance wound in the head but no exit wound and no bullet in the head. Lawyers for Panthers intimated that the missing bullet had been secretly extracted and disposed of by the police, because it constituted evidence of murder.

A third version was rendered by a federal grand jury that had been specially empaneled to investigate the December 4 shootings. After having all the physical evidence recovered by both the police and the Panthers analyzed by the FBI Laboratory in Washington and evaluating additional ballistic evidence uncovered by the FBI, and after hearing all the witnesses willing to testify, the grand jury concluded, among other things, that the Chicago police investigation of the raid was "so seriously deficient that it suggests purposeful malfeasance."

When Groth and Davis forced their way in through the inner door, according to the grand jury's assessment of the events, a 12-gauge slug was fired from inside the apartment and passed through that door as it swung open to a 45-degree angle. There were indications that the shotgun was no more than fifteen inches from the opening door. A 12-gauge slug found at the scene proved consistent with a shotgun that was next to Mark Clark's body and was stained with blood of Clark's type; the slug was also found to match the hole in the door. Moreover, an empty shell found nearby was "positively identified" as having come from the shotgun. Piecing together the physical evidence, the jury posited that Mark Clark, sitting behind the door, fired a shotgun blast through the door just as the police burst in. This, however, was the only shot that could be definitely traced to a Panther weapon.

The grand jury concluded that Groth and Davis apparently came in shooting, for one pistol shot had been fired through the door. Davis shot Clark, who was sitting behind the door holding a shotgun, and a woman then in the room, Brenda Harris, who was holding another shotgun. Minutes later, after the officers claimed they heard a shotgun blast from a bedroom adjacent to the living room, the wall between the living room and the bedroom was "stitched" with forty-two shots from a carbine and a submachine gun. One of these bullets passed through the first bedroom into a second bedroom, where it fatally wounded Fred Hampton in the right forehead. Another bullet, apparently from the same volley, since it was traveling at the same angle, struck Hampton in the right cheek, and another struck him in the left shoulder. This last, the only bullet recovered from his body, proved to be a .30-caliber bullet from Davis's carbine. Aside from Hampton and Clark, four of the seven other Panthers in the apartment, as well as one police officer, were wounded by police gunfire in less than twelve minutes after the raid began. Eighty-three empty shells and fifty-six bullets were recovered from the apartment by the police, the Panthers and the FBI, of which all but one shotgun slug and one shell had been fired from police weapons. Although the police steadfastly maintained that at least ten or fifteen shots were

fired at them by Panthers, a painstaking reconstruction by the grand jury suggests that following
the first shot by Clark, police entering from the
back of the apartment mistook Davis's and
Groth's shots in the front of the apartment for
Panther gunfire, and the police in the front of the
apartment similarly mistook the "return" fire
from the rear of the apartment for continuing re-
sistance. According to the grand jury's version,
the officers very probably fired through the living-
room wall under the erroneous impression that
they were in a gun battle with Panthers.

The grand jury also attempted to resolve conflicts between the findings of the Panthers' private
autopsy and those of the police autopsy by ordering Hampton's body exhumed and yet a third
autopsy performed, by an out-of-state medical examiner in the presence of both a Chicago pathologist from the coroner's office and a pathologist
retained by the Hampton family. Two points were
clarified by the third autopsy. First, despite the
statement of the Panthers' pathologist that there
was no exit wound for the fatal bullet that entered
Hampton's forehead, this autopsy plainly showed
an exit hole in front of the left ear when the side-
burns were shaved. Second, the Panthers' claim
that Hampton was heavily drugged with Seconal
before the shooting was not supported either by
this autopsy, which showed "no trace of drugs in
the body," or by the report of the FBI Laboratory
in Washington, which had also tested the sample
used in the Panthers' private autopsy. The toxicologist who performed the analysis for the Panthers told the grand jury that he had not per-

formed the most specific test for Seconal, the gas-chromatography test, but had relied instead on a less sophisticated test, which required some "subjective evaluation." In performing the gas-chromatography test on the same sample that the Panthers' toxicologist had used, the FBI found no Seconal or other drugs in the sample but did find deterioration in the blood that could have been partially responsible for a mistaken analysis.

On the basis of the grand jury's meticulous investigation of the killings, it seems reasonable to conclude that Hampton was fatally shot not while he was "drugged" or by a policeman standing over him with a silencer, as the Panthers have claimed, but by a bullet fired by a police officer in the living room which had passed through two intervening walls at a time when no Panthers were firing at police.

Are these ten cases of Black Panthers killed by police part of a nationally coordinated pattern? Although Hampton and Clark were the only Panthers killed as a direct result of a planned police raid, or even in a situation in which the police could reasonably be supposed to have had advance knowledge that they would confront Black Panthers, it still might be maintained that the police involved had instructions of some sort to kill Black Panthers whenever the opportunity presented itself. The theory broached by John Kifner in the *Times* that the Nixon administration had, through the statements of public officials, "at least contributed to a climate of opinion among local police . . . that a virtual open season has been declared on the Panthers" seems historically inaccurate, since five of the ten Panther deaths that can be directly attributed to police action occurred before the Nixon administration took office. And, as far as I have been able to determine, no Black Panthers have been killed by the police in the period of more than a year that has elapsed since the Hampton-Clark incident.

In all of the ten cases to which Garry's list has been reduced, at least some of the Panthers involved were armed and presented a threat to the police. Six of the ten Panthers were killed by seriously wounded policemen who clearly had reason to believe that their own lives were in jeopardy. In none of these cases, moreover, is there any positive evidence to support a belief that the wounded policemen knew they had been shot by Black Panthers. According to the evidence that *is* available, Bartholomew, Lawrence and Lewis were stopped as burglary suspects; Pope approached a robbery stakeout at night; Winters opened fire when two policemen entered an abandoned building to investigate a citizen's complaint; and although it is agreed that Roberson took it upon himself to challenge the behavior of the police investigating the burglary of a fruit stand, it is not reported that he identified himself as a Black Panther.

In the four remaining cases, the fatal shots were fired by policemen who had not themselves been wounded. A further distinction might be made to take account of the fact that in two of these deaths—those of Armstead and Clark—the police state that in each instance they were confronted by an adversary with a lethal weapon and had reason to presume that their own lives were

endangered. Armstead pointed a rifle at a policeman and refused to disarm himself; Clark confronted a policeman with a shotgun, which, in
fact, he had previously fired. In any event, there
are two cases in which Black Panthers were killed
by policemen whose lives were not being directly
threatened by those men. These are the cases of
Hutton, who was shot while allegedly running
from the scene of a ninety-minute gun battle in
which three policemen had been wounded, and
Hampton, who was apparently hit by stray bullets
in a reckless and uncontrolled fusillade.

Four deaths, two deaths, even a single death
must be the subject of the most serious concern.
But the basic issues of public policy presented by
the militancy of groups like the Panthers and by
the sometimes brutal police treatment of angry
and defiant black people in general can be neither
understood nor resolved in an atmosphere of exaggerated charges—whether of "genocide" against
the Panthers or of "guerrilla warfare" against the
police—that are repeated, unverified, in the press
and in consequence widely believed by the public.
The idea that the police have declared a sort of
open season on the Black Panthers is based princi-
pally, as far as I can determine, on the assumption
that all the Panther deaths cited by Charles Garry
—twenty-eight or twenty or ten—occurred under
circumstances that were similar to the Hampton-
Clark raid. This is an assumption that proves, on
examination, to be false.

—"The Panthers and the Police:
A Pattern of Genocide?"
The New Yorker, February 1971

THE
PENTAGON PAPERS:
REVISING HISTORY

Any large collection of data must usually be reduced to manageable proportions by a newspaper with only limited space. In selecting the information for publication, journalists must follow some criteria for editing and organizing the story. Frequently, the model employed is the duplicity theme in which information is selected that reveals the contradictions between what officials say in public and in private. The focus on duplicity tends, however, to neglect and even distort other interpretations of history. Consider the case of the Pentagon Papers.

On June 13, 1971, *The New York Times* announced in its Sunday edition that it had obtained a "massive study of how the United States went to war in Indochina" which had been secretly prepared by the Department of Defense in 1968, and thereupon began the series of reports about this secret study that was to earn for it the Pulitzer Prize for "service in the public interest." The Pentagon Papers, as the study was generally called, had been commissioned by Secretary of Defense Robert S. McNamara in 1967, and was undertaken by a group of anonymous analysts working under the direction of Leslie H. Gelb in the office of International Security Affairs of the Pentagon. The researchers were given access to the working files of the Secretary of Defense, as well as some State Department and CIA memorandums, and instructed to write from this material an "encyclopedic and objective" narrative history of the decisions that involved the United States in Indochina between 1940 and 1968. Thousands of classified documents were appended to the study to avoid the charge that the analysts had quoted the documents "out of context." Most of the resulting 7,000-page study was made available to the *Times* by Daniel Ellsberg, a former special assistant in the office of International Security Affairs, who had worked briefly on the project.

Despite unprecedented efforts by the Department of Justice to suppress the study on the grounds that its full publication would jeopardize "national security"—efforts which the *Times* courageously and successfully fought through the Supreme Court—the disclosures in the *Times* were reported in one form or another by virtually every major newspaper and broadcasting station in the country, and profoundly affected public opinion on the war. In light of these well-documented reports, it appeared that the tragic war in Vietnam could no longer simply be explained as a "quagmire" that the Kennedy and Johnson administrations were dragged into willy-nilly by circumstances and contingencies outside of their control. On the contrary, these disclosures now suggested that U.S. involvement was the product of a clique of willful men, who secretly led the nation into a full-scale war, even while denying this aim to the American public and Congress.

There was good reason to accept this version of history, if not as a final truth, at least as the closest approximation to it that the public was likely to receive. It derived from an archive of Defense Department documents meant only for the eyes of the top decision-makers in government. Not even future historians could be expected to have full access to such material as did the Pentagon analysts. Moreover, unlike government pronouncements and "leaks," which presumably are designed to serve some interested party, the Pentagon study was never meant for public release, and therefore there would be no prima facie reason to believe that the analysts would distort the record or conceal damaging information. To be sure, it was a study mainly limited to the records of a single government agency, the Department of Defense, but within these bounds, there was no reason to doubt that it was an accurate, even if possibly incomplete, history of the decisions about Vietnam.

The *Times* did not, however, publish the text of the Pentagon study itself (as it did with another famous government "leak," the Yalta Papers [March 17, 1955]), or even substantial parts of it. Instead, it published stories about the secret history, prepared by four *Times* reporters, Neil Sheehan, Hedrick Smith, E. W. Kenworthy, and Fox Butterfield, with the assistance of *Times* editors and researchers. As Max Frankel pointed out in the *Times* the following Sunday, "After months of painstaking research, analysis and preparation, the *Times* began last Sunday to give its readers a more orderly, though also more concise, rendering of the history than the study itself." It was these "renderings," rather than the actual text of the Pentagon study, that the *Times* and Bantam Books later published under the title *The Pentagon Papers*, and a selection of "key texts" taken from the study.

Although the *Times* never made public the text of the Pentagon study it described, the Beacon Press (a small nonprofit publishing house in Boston sponsored by the Unitarian Universalist Association) obtained a copy of the same secret study through the efforts of Senator Mike Gravel (Democrat, Alaska). Senator Gravel had obtained this Xeroxed copy at the time when the Nixon administration was attempting to stop the *Times'* publication of the study, and immediately entered large sections of the secret study in the *Congressional Record*. Then, with the cooperation of Senator Gravel, the Beacon Press decided to publish the bulk of the Pentagon study verbatim in four volumes. This was after a number of other publishing houses discreetly refused to undertake the publication.

In effect, then, the Beacon Press published

the actual text of the study from which the *Times* had derived its prize-winning reports. In comparing the *Times* reports with the actual text of the Pentagon study, however, it becomes clear that the *Times* version is something more than a simple paraphrasing of the secret history, or even an abridged "rendering." Substantial revisions in the history were made on major points. The extent to which the history was revised can be seen from the *Times'* treatment of the Pentagon study's findings about the decision to bomb North Vietnam. The front-page story on June 14, which the *Times* identified as a "major disclosure," began:

VIETNAM ARCHIVE:
A CONSENSUS TO BOMB DEVELOPED
BEFORE '64 ELECTION, STUDY SAYS

The Johnson Administration reached a "general consensus" at a White House strategy meeting on Sept. 7, 1964, that air attacks against North Vietnam would probably have to be launched, a Pentagon study of the Vietnam war states. It was expected that "these operations would begin early in the year" . . . The administration consensus on bombing came at the height of the Presidential election contest between President Johnson and Senator Barry Goldwater, whose advocacy of full-scale air attacks on North Vietnam had become a major issue. That such a consensus had been reached as early as September is a major disclosure of the Pentagon study.

The implications were stunning: President Johnson had secretly decided to bomb North Vietnam at a time when he was publicly calling for no wider war in Vietnam. Such a gross deception could hardly be ignored by editorial writers and columnists. Tom Wicker, in his column of June 20 in the *Times,* for example, contrasted President Johnson's speech of September 28, 1964, in which he said, "We are not going North and drop bombs at this stage of the game," with the Pentagon study, which he noted said that "Mr. Johnson and his advisors had reached on Sept. 7, 1964, what the Pentagon's own historical study of these events terms a general consensus that air attacks would have to be launched against North Vietnam." While several publications, notably *Newsweek, Time* and the *Wall Street Journal,* raised some questions about the validity of this harsh judgment in the light of other available evidence —including even some of the documents the *Times* appended to its reports—it was difficult to deny the cogency of "the Pentagon's own historical study."

From the Beacon edition, however, it becomes clear that the Pentagon study did not so clearly reach the conclusions that the *Times* specifically attributed to it. Rather than stating that "the Johnson Administration reached a 'general consensus' at a White House strategy meeting on Sept. 7, 1964, that air attacks against North Vietnam would probably have to be launched," the only statement in the Pentagon study which uses the quoted phrase "general consensus" in reference to the September 7 meeting, reads, "By early September, a general consensus had developed among high-level administration officials" in the entire Johnson administration, and he [Johnson] escalated "some form" of pressure into "air attacks against North Vietnam." While the study

carefully traces out from documents how State
and Defense Department officials dealing with Vietnam in 1964 became convinced as the year pro-
gressed that the fighting in South Vietnam was
subjected to some diplomatic and military pressures, it also makes it abundantly clear that a
whole range of pressures was being actively considered—including deploying American ships in
Vietnamese waters, air reconnaisance over Laos,
South Vietnamese interdiction of infiltration
routes in Laos, "deliberately provocative actions,"
and enlisting the help of allies in Southeast Asia
to isolate North Vietnam—aside from direct air
attacks on North Vietnam.

Specifically, at the September "strategy meeting" referred to in the *Times,* the principal con-
ferees, which included the President, Secretary of
State Dean Rusk, Secretary of Defense Robert
McNamara, General Earle G. Wheeler, of the
Joint Chiefs of Staff, and CIA Director John
McCone, rejected, rather than accepted, the proposal of the Joint Chiefs for an immediate bombing campaign against the North. The Pentagon
study itself states:

The reasons cited for their opposition to provocative acts were also applied in *rejecting* proposals for an
immediate bombing campaign. The GVN (Govern-
ment of South Vietnam) was expected to be too weak
for the United States to assume the "deliberate risks of
escalation that would involve a major role for, or threat
to, South Vietnam." In the discussion, Mr. McCone
observed that undertaking a sustained attack on the
DRV (North Vietnam) would be very dangerous, due
to the weakness and unpredictability of the political

base in South Vietnam. Secretary Rusk stated the view
that every means short of bombing must be exhausted.

The consensus reached at this meeting was,
in fact, to apply pressures *other* than bombing to
North Vietnam, according to the study, which
concluded:

Even though the principals did not accept the JCS
(Joint Chiefs of Staff) proposal and apparently did not
agree with their assessment of the chances for improve-
ment in South Vietnam, they did indicate accord with
the JCS sense of the gravity of the U.S. predicament.

And therefore:

The meeting resulted in consensus among the principals on certain courses of prompt action to put additional pressure on North Vietnam. The following mea-
sures were recommended to the President for his
decision:
  1. U.S. naval patrols in the Gulf of Tonkin should be
resumed immediately. . . .
  2. 34A operations by the GVN should be resumed
immediately thereafter. . . .
  3. Limited GVN air and ground operations into the
corridor areas of Laos should be undertaken in the near
future . . . as soon as we can get [Premier] Souvanna's
permission. . . .
  4. We should be *prepared* to respond on a tit-for-tat
basis against the DRV[against specific and related tar-
gets] in the event of any attack on U.S. units or any
special DRV/VC action against SVN.

None of the actions recommended by the
"consensus" at the September 7 meeting involved
American bombing of North Vietnam. The naval
patrols in international waters off the coast of

North Vietnam, which were intended mainly as a show of force and a means of monitoring North Vietnamese communications, were being resumed after the North Vietnamese torpedo attack a few weeks earlier. The covert South Vietnamese maritime operations, code-named "34A," which were an effort to disrupt the flow of arms into South Vietnam, were simply being resumed after a temporary suspension. And South Vietnamese actions in Laos were intended primarily as a warning to North Vietnam, according to the Pentagon study. The only new recommendation was for preparing an American capacity to retaliate if attacked. This did not necessarily mean that retaliatory raids would be ordered; indeed, despite the strong recommendations of the American mission for reprisals for two attacks that did occur in 1964, President Johnson refused to effect them. In the case of the first attack, the November 1 bombing of the American airbase at Bien Hoa, the Pentagon study notes, "Concerned about possible further North Vietnamese escalation and the uncertainty of the Red Chinese response, the White House decides, against the advice of Ambassador Taylor, not to retaliate." In the second case, the Christmas Eve attack on American barracks in Saigon, the study concludes, "At the meeting of the NSC [National Security Council] principals, a decision against reprisals for the barracks bombing is taken in spite of the strong recommendations" for it by Ambassador [Maxwell] Taylor and the Joint Chiefs of Staff."

The Presidential decision on these proposed recommendations was issued three days later, on

September 10, in National Security Action Memorandum No. 314. It again specifically excluded the bombing of the North, even as a covert operation by the South Vietnamese. The study calls attention to this, stating, "It is significant that although this order, in effect, authorized the initiation of Phase III (October through December) of the covert operations under OPERATIONS PLAN 34A, it specified contrary to the provisions of Phase III that 'we should not consider air strikes under 34A for the present.' "

Although the *Times* asserted in its story that the "general consensus" to bomb North Vietnam was "reflected" in the "final paragraph" of this memorandum, which "spoke of 'larger decisions' which might be required at any time," the final paragraph does not necessarily support such a conclusion when it is read in full context:

These decisions are governed by a prevailing judgment that the first order of business at present is to take actions which will help to strengthen the fabric of the Government of South Vietnam; to the extent that the situation permits, such action should precede larger decisions. If such larger decisions are required at any time by a change in the situation, they will be taken.

In other words, the President *declined* to make any larger decisions about future escalations at that time.

In the text of the Pentagon study itself, the chronology of the decision to bomb the North is fairly well established. As late as December 1964, the study states, "It is clear that the President did not make any commitment at this point to expand the war through future operations against North Vietnam," and places these decisions to escalate the war through bombing "in the early months of 1965."

In addition to revising the history so that it appeared that these decisions were made before the Presidential election in 1964, the *Times* also revised other pertinent facts. Consider, for example, the disparate descriptions of the National Security Council study, which was initiated on November 3, 1964. The *Times* stated in its (June 14, 1971) story, "The last round of detailed planning of various political and military strategies for a bombing campaign began 'in earnest,' the study says, on November 3rd, 1964, the day that Mr. Johnson was elected President in his own right." This, of course, is consistent with the thesis that a decision had been made in September to bomb the North. On the other hand, the Pentagon history put the November 3 study in a completely different context, stating:

> The President was not ready to approve a program of air strikes against North Vietnam, at least until the available alternatives could be carefully and thoroughly re-examined.
> Such a re-examination was initiated immediately following the election, under the aegis of a NSC interagency working group chaired by Assistant Secretary of State William Bundy.

According to the Pentagon study, none of the tasks of this study group included planning strategies for a bombing campaign.

There is no reason to presume that this rewriting was a purposeful or in any way malicious attempt to falsify the then secret history. The search for duplicity in the conduct of public affairs has been a traditional and respected focus of American journalism. This is especially true in the area of foreign affairs, where it is commonly presumed that official explanations for policies are no more than convenient rationales for Realpolitik reasons of state which are never voluntarily divulged. Exposing the presumed disparity between what political leaders say in public and in private is therefore generally regarded as one of the highest forms of journalism. (Jack Anderson, the syndicated columnist, also won a Pulitzer Prize in 1972 for revealing the secret deliberations of Presidential adviser Henry Kissinger over the India–Pakistan war.) It is not surprising then that the *Times* attempted to organize the secret archive it had received in terms of the duplicity theme; or that it listed what it considered to be the most dramatic disclosures of the Pentagon study—including the preelection "general consensus" to bomb the North—in a special box entitled "What They Said in Public and in Private."

The Pentagon study, however, was not primarily concerned with duplicity. It was a Department of Defense study, done by analysts closely connected with the government of the decision-making process in the Vietnamese involvement. The *Times* thus had the problem of converting a bureaucratic study into a journalistic exposé, and this required substantial reorganization of the history and the addition of outside material. The effects of this conversion can be clearly seen by comparing the different treatments of the Tonkin Gulf incidents that led to bombing reprisals in the summer of 1964. In the Pentagon study itself, no support is given to the widely voiced suspicions that the Johnson administration either fabricated or deliberately provoked the putative attacks on American destroyers in the Gulf of Tonkin so that Congress could be stampeded into passing a resolution supporting the war. In the case of the first incident, on July 31, the Pentagon study finds that the American destroyer U.S.S. *Maddox* was attacked by three North Vietnamese patrol boats in broad daylight at a time when the American ship was "28 miles from the coast [of North Vietnam] and heading farther into international waters." While the study suggests the possibility that the North Vietnamese might have "mistaken *Maddox* for a South Vietnamese escort vessel" that had been involved in a clandestine raid on North Vietnamese islands on the previous night, it concludes that the American destroyer had not deliberately provoked the incident or had been involved in the South Vietnamese raid.

The second attack, which occurred on August 4, was the more controversial incident. Since it provided a basis for the first American bombing reprisal of North Vietnam and the congressional resolution authorizing the President to take whatever actions were necessary to defend the American position in Vietnam, there was considerable speculation that this second incident might have been either entirely fabricated or deliberately provoked in order to justify an escalation of the war.

Indeed, in 1969, the Senate Foreign Relations Committee investigated the incidents without being able to satisfactorily dispel these doubts. The Pentagon study, however, reached conclusions that closely supported the administration's version of the incident:

> The reality of a North Vietnamese attack on 4 August has been corroborated by both visual and technical evidence. That it may have been deliberately provoked by the United States is belied to a considerable degree by circumstantial evidence.

For example, the Pentagon study concluded that stricter operating restrictions for the destroyers in international waters after the first incident "indicates an intention to avoid—not provoke— further contact." And noting that the North Vietnamese PT boats attempted what seemed to be a planned "ambushing" of the U.S. destroyers, it further concluded, "The ways in which the events of the second Tonkin Gulf incident came about give little indication of a deliberate provocation to provide opportunity for reprisals."

The version found in the *Times* is quite different. The conclusion of the Pentagon study that the Tonkin attacks were not deliberately provoked by the United States is not quoted in the *Times* account. On the contrary, the *Times*' story strongly suggests that both Tonkin incidents might have been provoked by clandestine operations against North Vietnam by the United States (the incident that the *Times* suggested might have provoked the second North Vietnam PT attack, a bombing of North Vietnamese villages just across the Laotian border, is not even mentioned in the text of the Pentagon study). "When the Tonkin incident occurred," the *Times* reported, "the Johnson Administration did not reveal these clandestine attacks, and pushed the previously prepared resolution through both houses of Congress on Aug. 7." The central issue in the *Times* was again converted to one of deception, or the failure to reveal secrets to the public. This was not, in fact, an issue in the Pentagon study's treatment of the Tonkin incidents, but the *Times* made it an issue by adding pages of testimony from congressional testimony and press statements, which tended to demonstrate that Secretary McNamara had been deceptive in not revealing to Congress and the press the full extent of the South Vietnamese covert operations under American sponsorship. In this instance, the *Times* report may well have been neither irrelevant nor inaccurate, but still it diverged substantially from the history it was purportedly reporting on.

Certainly, the relentless pursuit of official deception is one of the more important services rendered by journalism in a democracy, and the *Times* was within this tradition in developing the duplicity theme in the Pentagon study. The Pentagon study, however, deserves to be read in its own right: it is not only a uniquely documented study of the chain of decisions that led to the enormous tragedy in Vietnam, but also, in meticulously analyzing the misjudgments, misinterpretations, and mistaken priorities that lay behind them, a revelation of a certain pathology of power. At the root of the problem was a supreme commitment to the infallibility of rational planning. Most of the civilian decision-makers shared the belief that the United States could compel North Vietnam to modify basic national policies through a well-orchestrated program of pressures that would fall short of all-out warfare, or even a "wider war" in Asia. The assumption that the consequences of these "graduated pressures" could be anticipated and controlled runs paramount in the scenarios, contingency plans, interagency studies, and policy memorandums during the early years (1963–1966) of the war, which were the main subject of the Pentagon history. Since it was clear by the time Secretary McNamara commissioned the study in 1967 that the planning had egregiously failed to achieve objectives or foresee the consequences of the escalations, it became incumbent on the writers of the Pentagon study to explain the failure of rational planning in Vietnam. Such failures could not be explained simply in terms of the deception of the American public, but required a fuller examination of the processes by which information is evaluated, objectives are defined, and decisions are reached. In attempting to analyze these processes, with vastly greater access to government secret documents and working papers than had previously been available to historians, the Pentagon study raised some basic questions about the inherent limits of this sort of rational planning in the conduct of foreign policy.

First, there is the problem of imposing a model of rationality on the expected behavior of an enemy who has an entirely different set of interests at stake, and therefore, different perceptions

of the conflict. The Pentagon study thus points to
the repeated failure of the United States to "signal" its true intentions to North Vietnam. For
example, most of the clandestine military actions
in 1964 that the *Times* depicted as a "covert war"
were characterized by the Pentagon study itself as
"signals" that were "intended more to demonstrate U.S. resolve than to affect the military situation." The study states, "Throughout 1964, a basic U.S. policy in Vietnam was to severely restrain
any expansion of the direct U.S. combat involvement, but to carry out an essentially psychological
campaign to convince Hanoi that the United
States meant business." Yet the destroyer patrols
in the Gulf of Tonkin, the commando raids on
North Vietnam, and the armed reconnaissance
over Laos, which were all part of this "psychological campaign," were apparently interpreted either
as direct provocations or, ironically, as signs of a
lack of United States commitment by North Vietnam, which progressively intensified its support of
the insurgency in South Vietnam throughout
1964. The National Security Council's "working
group" on Vietnam presumed that the introduc-
tion of U.S. jets into Laos in late 1964 would be
viewed by Hanoi as a major U.S. commitment, but
Hanoi apparently misread the "signal." The Pentagon study notes that Defense officials asked for
an evaluation of this operation in Laos, code-
named BARREL ROLL, because neither the North
Vietnamese nor Chinese Communists had made
any public mention or "appeared to have taken
cognizance of our BARREL ROLL operations." "In
response," the study continues, "a DIA [Defense

Intelligence Agency] assessment indicated that the Communists apparently had made no 'distinction between BARREL ROLL missions on the one hand and the Laotian T-28 (jet) strikes and YANKEE TEAM missions [which involved jets flown by Thai mercenaries] on the other.' Attributing all stepped-up operations in Laos to the United States and its 'lackeys,' they had lumped all operations together." In this and other instances, the expectation of American planners that the North Vietnamese would distinguish among the ascending steps in the scenario of escalation assumed that Hanoi would conform to the American model of rationality. Viewed from a different perspective, however, escalations such as the use of American pilots in Laos could be interpreted as just another half-hearted attempt to harass North Vietnamese supply lines in Laos—or as an "irrational" provocation. That North Vietnam treated such signals in the "psychological campaign" as simple military interventions (assuming they were noticed at all), which required further force on their part, rather than as subtle attempts at communication, indicated the extent to which such highly sophisticated planning was vulnerable to misinterpretation by a less "sophisticated" enemy.

An even more serious problem for the American planners lay in accurately interpreting the intentions and actions of the North Vietnamese. In keeping with its theme of deception, the *Times'* version suggests that virtually all CIA reports revealed the futility of the policy of bombing North Vietnam, but that the principal advisers refused to "reshape their policy" accordingly, and continued to maintain publicly that the bombing was effective. For example, in regard to the critical expansion of the air war to Hanoi and Haiphong in 1966, the *Times* asserted: ". . . the study discloses that the [Johnson] Administration's decision in 1966 to bomb North Vietnam's oil storage facilities was made despite repeated warnings from the Central Intelligence Agency that such action would not 'cripple Communist military operations.' " The Pentagon study itself, however, suggests that intelligence evaluations by the CIA and other agencies were considerably more ambiguous and contradictory on this point. While the CIA concluded in reports dated November 27 and December 3 that attacks on petroleum storage at Haiphong and elsewhere were unlikely to "cripple" North Vietnam's efforts in South Vietnam, it revised its conclusion in a December 28 report, claiming now that bombing these targets would "curtail the output of the DRV's modest industrial establishment and complicate the problems of internal distribution" and thereby make it more difficult to support the war in the South. Moreover, the Pentagon study states, the other intelligence agencies, with the exception of the State Department, looked "with favor upon escalating the bombing." By March 1967 the CIA strongly endorsed the escalation. The study states in a section entitled "The CIA Recommends Escalation" that the March report

virtually wrote off the bombing results to date as insignificant, in terms of either interdiction or pressure; blamed "the highly restrictive ground rules" under which the [bombing] program operated; and took the bold step, for an intelligence document, of explicitly recommending a preferred bombing program of greater intensity, redirected largely against "the will of the regime as a target system."

This March CIA report was extremely "influential," according to the Pentagon study. Not only did it strengthen the Joint Chiefs of Staff's "proposals to intensify the bombing," but, in particular, "the report gave a substantial boost to the proposal to hit the POL [petroleum, oil, lubricants] targets," which was then approved.

The subsequent failure of the bombing of the oil facilities to achieve, even in military terms, the results predicted by the intelligence services raised serious questions about the reliability of the U.S. intelligence system in Vietnam (rather than, as the *Times* implied, the willingness of the planners to abide by intelligence estimates). To some degree, the intelligence failure is part of the more general problem of intelligence forecasting, which Roberta Wohlstetter delineated in her classic study of the difficulties in anticipating the attack at Pearl Harbor despite numerous warnings. Intelligence "signals" always tend to be ambiguous and uncertain. As information is passed upwards in an intelligence system, judgments must be made at each level as to what represents relevant information and what represents "noise"—inaccurate or irrelevant information. In reaching a high-level consensus, conflicts and ambiguities must then be ironed out of the lower-level reports, according to which assessment seems to dovetail most closely with the general view of a situation, or what is considered to be the most plausible possibility. The highest-level intelligence reports are thus always vulnerable to major errors—especially if the prevailing view is faulty in some respect.

In Vietnam, the intelligence problem was made acutely more difficult by the fact that the American objectives were essentially psychological rather than physical. As the Pentagon study notes, "the real target was the *will* of the North Vietnamese government to continue the aggression in the South rather than its *capability* to do so." In these circumstances, intelligence agencies had to predict and assess results in psychological terms—for example, whether the bombing of the Haiphong oil facilities would "break" or strengthen North Vietnamese resolve. This obviously is a much more speculative enterprise than predicting the physical damage that a bombing campaign might accomplish—and even that was not always done with a great degree of accuracy —because it requires making judgments about the thinking of North Vietnam leaders.

The attempt at rationally planning a limited conflict in Vietnam was further frustrated by the complex international situation on which it was dependent. Each direct action against North Vietnam could be expected to have repercussions on Sino-Soviet relations, United States-Soviet relations, North Vietnamese-Soviet relations, and a number of other matters that could not be precisely determined. Yet these secondary effects, no matter how indeterminate they were, had to be entered in the calculus. For example, in late 1964 the National Security Council's "working group" on Vietnam, after a complicated analysis of the triangular relations among China, the Soviet Union, and North Vietnam, concluded:

Moscow's *ability* to influence decisions in Hanoi tends [because of the need for Soviet military aid] "consequently" to be proportional to the North Vietnamese regime's fears of American action against it, rising in moments of crisis and diminishing in quieter periods. Moscow's *willingness* to give overt backing to Hanoi, however, seems to be in inverse proportion to the level of threat to North Vietnam.

Under this logic, presumably a high level of threats, such as bombing, would both increase the Soviets' influence in Hanoi (vis-à-vis China's) and, at the same time, lessen their willingness to aid Hanoi. Since these were both American objectives at the time, this analysis, based on highly speculative assumptions, became a strong argument for increasing the military pressure against North Vietnam. In retrospect, of course, the assumptions proved wrong, and the Soviet Union increased its military aid to Hanoi without apparently using any of the increased influence it might have gained for resolving the conflict. Strategic planning that had of necessity to be predicated not only on how an enemy would react but on how third parties such as the Soviet Union and China would react was problematic at best.

While the Pentagon study was never meant as a definitive analysis of the tragedy of Vietnam, but only (in the words of its editor) as an "input into the history," it provides a rare insight into the strategic thinking and processes that helped formulate America's Vietnam policy. No doubt future historians will make different assessments of the basic facts in the documents and future political scientists will draw different lessons from them. Yet, for the moment, it is the revised version of history, organized along the lines of the duplicity theme, which *The New York Times* and other journals have made available to the public.

—1972

THE CORNFELD FOLLIES: THE PROBLEM OF FINANCIAL REPORTING

The American tradition of muckraking, which got its formal designation in 1906, when Theodore Roosevelt used the term to disparage writers who specialized in exposing corruption, was at first concentrated more on the misdeeds of business than on those of government. In the early years of the century, the best investigative reporting was found in such attacks on unfettered private enterprise as Ida M. Tarbell's *The History of the Standard Oil Company*, Charles P. Norcross's *The Rebate Conspiracy*, Judson C. Welliver's *The Mormon Church and the Sugar Trust*, Upton Sinclair's *The Condemned Meat Industry*, and Louis D. Brandeis's *The Greatest Insurance Wrong*. In more recent years, however, the muckrakers, with the significant exception of Ralph Nader, seem to have turned away from corporate abuses in favor of searching out political corruption. Since 1917, when the first Pulitzer Prizes were announced, nearly three times as many have been awarded for exposing political corruption of one sort or another as for reporting on activities of the business community.

This preoccupation can be explained partly in terms of risk: publishing political exposés carries with it comparatively little chance of litigation, especially now that Supreme Court decisions have made it virtually impossible for public figures to obtain damages for libel unless there is proof of deliberate malice. There is also the matter of access: information is less readily available from private corporations than from government agencies, which employ platoons of press officers, not to mention a number of dissident bureaucrats. Moreover, nearly all information about governmental transactions is presumed to be in the public domain, if only it can be ferreted out. In the controversy over the publication of the Pentagon Papers by *The New York Times* and other newspapers, a number of eminent journalists took the position that revealing government secrets, even classified ones, can be a vital part—indeed, a responsibility —of the reporter's job. On the other hand, disclosing corporate secrets, especially where such information might help a company's competitors, is not an accepted practice among journalists. Such important corporate secrets as pricing arrangements, marketing plans, contract bids, and even strategies for the planned obsolescence of products or for the circumvention of public policies have rarely been revealed in the press.

In the political world, the journalist has a relatively uncomplicated notion of what constitutes corruption. Any public official who benefits financially from surreptitious or unorthodox practices is under suspicion, even if there is no actual violation of the law. For example, Abe Fortas was forced to resign from the Supreme Court when *Life* revealed that he had been paid $20,000 as a "consultant" by a private foundation set up by Louis Wolfson, who was in prison for selling unregistered securities. No one charged that Fortas had violated any law, had made a quid-pro-quo deal with Wolfson in order to get the money, or had intervened in any legal proceedings against Wolfson; in fact, Fortas had disqualified himself from sitting on any case connected with Wolfson, and Wolfson had received a fairly stiff sentence. But, as the *Times* said in an editorial, "serious questions of propriety" were raised, so Fortas had to resign.

Financiers and industrialists, on the other hand, are expected to make large personal profits from unorthodox and secret transactions. Howard Hughes, Hugh Hefner, Aristotle Onassis and J. Paul Getty have been lionized in the press for their mysterious business skills. In the corporate realm, not even deliberate deception is necessarily considered evidence of corruption. Businesses quite commonly use ingenious bookkeeping devices to make their earnings appear more or less than they actually are, for the purpose of avoiding taxes, of enhancing a labor-negotiating position, or simply of inflating the price of a stock. Inventories are unrealistically evaluated, assets are transferred from one subsidiary to another by artificial internal charges, and ownership is converted to rental through sale and leaseback agreements. The *Wall Street Journal* and a few specialized financial periodicals have run reports on this sort of manipulation, but in general the daily press gives it no attention unless it is in direct and unambiguous violation of the law. Even when there are colossal corporate failures affecting our entire society, such as the bankruptcy of the Penn Central, the press tends to concentrate on mismanagement rather than on the possibility of skulduggery as the explanation.

The difficulties and shortcomings of American reporting on business activities are well illustrated by the contrast between the coverage in the domestic press of the rise and fall of Investors Overseas Services (I.O.S.), a $2 billion financial complex that was founded in 1956 by Bernard Cornfeld, and the carefully documented account of the same events that has appeared in the recent book *Do You Sincerely Want to Be Rich?* by three British writers, Charles Raw, Bruce Page, and Godfrey Hodgson. Cornfeld, who grew up in Brooklyn, had held a number of jobs, including that of social worker, before he began his career in international finance. Under his direction, I.O.S. eventually owned and managed about a dozen mutual funds of the sort that are called "offshore," because they are registered in countries like Luxembourg and Panama, where they not only avoid taxes but are effectively free of regulations that more traditional business ventures must observe. In *Fortune* for March 1968, Martin Mayer called I.O.S.'s most spectacular mutual fund, the Fund of Funds, "a stroke of genius." He went on to describe a number of aggressive and sometimes "barely legal" tactics that were to make I.O.S. notorious, but nevertheless concluded, "Cornfeld has demonstrated that there are great pools of potential investment capital available in all the European countries for people who will go out and solicit it. The European banks, however distasteful they find Cornfeld's American methods, will not long allow their fastidiousness to fence them off from the exploitation of this gold mine. . . . The real significance of the I.O.S. invasion is that it is creating a major new market for equity capital in Europe." The *Fortune* article was generally skeptical in tone, but in July 1969 a rather breathless story in *Newsweek* entitled "Bernie and His Billions" described Cornfeld as "a self-made emperor of international finance," whose "genius had created the largest financial sales organization in the world." Two pages of color photographs of various aspects of his imperial "life style"—châteaus, banquets and "an endless succession of swinging girl friends"—testified to his personal financial success; a chart mapped out the extent of his company's fiduciary power and influence; and the magazine commented with wonder on Cornfeld's "ability to sell his 20,000 employees on the conviction that I.O.S. is saving capitalism and improving *la condition*

humaine." In January 1970 an article in *Time*
entitled "The Midas of Mutual Funds" declared,
"I.O.S. has prospered by flouting tradition and
stretching laws to their limit. Yet Cornfeld has
popularized equity investment in Europe and, in
the scramble to compete with him, a whole conti-
nent is beginning to turn towards the 'people's
capitalism' that Cornfeld preaches. Cornfeld's in-
novating has produced problems and controversy,
but so far the benefits have outweighed the troubles."

The troubles of I.O.S. included a set-to with
the Securities and Exchange Commission, which
in February 1966 had disclosed, after a year's
investigation by government lawyers, that the
company had made misleading and deceptive
statements in its solicitations for funds and had
arranged for rebates on commissions earned by
brokers without passing on anything to the mutual
funds for which the transactions had been made;
the S.E.C. also charged I.O.S. with selling shares
in its Fund of Funds in the United States, even
though it was not registered here. Finally, in May
1967, I.O.S. consented to conduct no further dealings under the jurisdiction of the S.E.C. *Newsweek*
mentioned in its July 1969 story that I.O.S. had
"tangled with . . . the U.S. Securities and Exchange Commission"—in a paragraph that began,
"The impetuous Cornfeld has put together this
empire in the face of the persistent antagonism of
foreign financial institutions, which dislike his
brash American sales techniques, and many foreign governments, which dislike his organization's
occasional bending of their laws." More specifi-

cally, the *Newsweek* article noted that the S.E.C. had "complained about corner-cutting in I.O.S.'s dealings on U.S. securities markets and charged that I.O.S. was illegally selling unregistered securities to U.S. investors," and went on to say that the S.E.C. was "particularly frustrated by the fact that I.O.S. was operating in ways that would have been illegal if I.O.S. had been a U.S.-based company." The fact that I.O.S. was operating "offshore," out of reach of government regulations, was, *Newsweek* suggested, what allowed it to be "so successful at sheltering its income" from taxes. And *Business Week,* in an article in January 1970 entitled "Bernie Cornfeld: King of Europe's Cash," declared it to be the belief of the financial community that, given his resources, "Cornfeld can take I.O.S. just about anywhere he wants."

The financial community was apparently wrong, however—as were a number of financial reporters—for by the spring of 1970 I.O.S. was in deep trouble. Cornfeld and his principal executives were being expelled from I.O.S. or were resigning; the price of I.O.S. stock had fallen from a high of $19.75 a share to less than $2; redemptions of the mutual-fund shares were exceeding purchases by anywhere from $2 million to $4 million a day; and I.O.S. salesmen were quitting in large numbers. In the course of a crisis that was threatening to produce serious repercussions in many European financial markets, it was revealed episodically in the press that I.O.S.'s management had manipulated the price of some essentially worthless oil-and-gas-exploration rights in the Arctic, thus artificially inflating the price of some of its mutual-fund shares; had drained off a large proportion of I.O.S.'s capital in the form of personal loans; and had made a number of highly misleading statements about the company's financial condition.

Even at this point, a relatively attentive reader might have concluded that the troubles of I.O.S. were a result solely of inefficient management rather than of any sort of malfeasance. On May 23, 1970, a feature story in the New York *Post,* devoted mostly to Cornfeld's life style, contained this evaluation of the expulsions and resignations: "The great bear market on Wall St. and the failure of his free-wheeling management to control costs are generally offered as explanations for Cornfeld's fall." Among a number of reports in the *Times* on I.O.S., one that appeared on May 11 and was entitled "How Cornfeld Lost His Empire" attributed I.O.S.'s difficulties not only to "financial razzle dazzle that raised eyebrows of more conservative financiers" but also, in part, to "the inability of management to control expenses" and "its somewhat unorthodox financial practices," which "left the company exposed as the great bear market set in on Wall Street." In the issue of *Newsweek* for July 6, 1970, a "Behind-Scenes Story" asserted that while I.O.S. funds "had encountered prolonged squalls in which clients redeemed more shares than they bought . . . the problem was in large part a crisis in confidence alone," and went on to say that "confidence seems to be slowly rebuilding." What was the cause of the crisis in confidence? According to *Newsweek,* "what made I.O.S. vulnerable was in

large part its sheer complexity," for "the bookkeeping was so tangled that its executives had no
convenient way to keep track of actual cash flow."
In September 1970, *Fortune* ran an article entitled
"Bernie Cornfeld: The Salesman Who Believed
Himself," which explained the I.O.S. collapse as
follows: "The cause was not the management of
I.O.S. fund assets, though errors of judgment were
made in this area, nor financial hanky-panky by
officers and directors, though insider loans were
made that were ethically questionable and wholly
inexcusable in the light of the liquidity crisis I.O.S.
was entering. The root cause was simply appall-
ingly bad management."

If columns of news space constitute a fair
measure, the American press was far more interested in reporting Cornfeld's colorful personal life
than in exploring his manipulations. Shortly after
he was forced to resign from the chairmanship
(but not from the board) of I.O.S., in May 1970 a
Times dispatch from Geneva by Bernard Wein-
raub under the head "Cornfeld, a Tycoon Bereft
of His Empire" began, "Bernard Cornfeld, who
was ousted last week as head of the problem-rid-
den mutual-fund empire he had erected, remains
locked in the 20-room villa built here by Napoleon
for Josephine, in the company of half a dozen
security men, four Great Danes, three eye-filling
women in their early twenties, two ocelots, a bas-
set hound and his 82-year-old mother." There followed details of his diet ("Hot pastrami and
salami are flown in on schedule from New York"),
his emotional state ("In the evenings, however,
the one-time Coney Island pitchman turned

supersalesman tends to become moody and melancholy"), and his favorite personal possessions ("He still has a private Mystère jet, a 13th-century castle in the French Alps, a London townhouse, a Paris apartment, a suite at the Hotel Carlyle in Manhattan, and a series of Rolls-Royces and Cadillacs"). Nothing was said in the article about how some of Cornfeld's possessions were acquired. Raw, Page, and Hodgson report that one of his planes—a BAC-111—was financed by a personal loan of $4.5 million from a bank that I.O.S. happened to own, and that the Carlyle suite was paid for by Arthur Lipper III, the head of a New York brokerage firm that, according to an S.E.C. examiner, had split commissions received on trading in I.O.S.'s mutual funds with Investors Planning Corporation, then owned by I.O.S. The *Times* dispatch from Geneva attributed the I.O.S. crisis to "spiraling expenses, declining income, questionable accounting practices and an expected first-quarter loss." Even the *Wall Street Journal,* which reported Cornfeld's manipulations in more detail than any other American newspaper, was explaining to its readers on June 11, 1970, that while a number of I.O.S. transactions raised ethical questions, "mismanagement rather than conscious irregularity brought the company to the edge of disaster," and that its dealings "suggest an operation more muddled than sordid, more the triumph of a salesman's super-optimism over the sober judgment that should have prevailed."

A very different explanation of I.O.S.'s troubles is offered by Raw, Page, and Hodgson. The thesis of *Do You Sincerely Want to Be Rich?* is set forth in no uncertain terms right at the beginning: "I.O.S. was not a respectable financial institution. It was an international swindle," and was "steeped in financial and intellectual dishonesty." British libel laws are strict, and charges like that require a considerable amount of documentation. Working very much in the tradition of the early muckrakers, and with the assistance of a full-time researcher and the part-time services of a number of other British correspondents, the authors, financed by the London *Sunday Times,* spent almost a year on their investigation, tracking down former employees of the far-flung I.O.S. empire and analyzing the endless financial statements and press releases that I.O.S. and its subsidiaries had issued.

One of Cornfeld's most recondite manipulations involved the revaluation of oil-and-gas-exploration rights in the Canadian Arctic that had been purchased by one of his mutual funds. On May 11, 1970, *The New York Times,* in its article explaining the collapse of I.O.S., stated that I.O.S.'s "Fund of Funds acquired half ownership of 22 million acres of Canadian Arctic land initially valued at $1 an acre," and went on to say, "Later, one million acres were sold for $14 an acre. The value of the rest of the holdings was then arbitrarily lifted to $8 an acre, which automatically increased the Fund of Funds asset value." The next day, another *Times* article stated that one of I.O.S.'s "most promising ventures" was still the "rights to millions of acres of potentially valuable Canadian Arctic lands near the oil-rich North Slope." Neither I.O.S. nor its Fund of

Funds ever acquired ownership of or leasehold on any land in the Canadian Arctic. What Cornfeld did acquire for the Fund of Funds, as the authors of *Do You Sincerely Want to Be Rich?* make clear, was an interest in some permits to explore vast stretches of the Arctic for specified mineral resources. The Canadian government makes such permits available at no cost to any company that promises to explore and develop the area—a requirement that is expressed as a cost per acre. Should the company strike oil and wish to convert its permits into leases, it may do so, subject to the Canadian government's right to keep half the acreage and to its requirement that at least half of the company's capital be owned by Canadians. Moreover, the land referred to in the *Times* article was not exactly in close proximity to the "oil-rich North Slope" of Alaska; the permits covered portions of the Arctic about twelve hundred miles from the parts of the North Slope where oil had been found. Strictly speaking, most of the "potentially valuable Canadian Arctic lands" weren't lands at all, since four-fifths of the area was under either frozen ocean or permanent ice cap. Drilling would have been difficult, to put it mildly.

In a sense, it was correct to describe the rights as "initially valued at $1 an acre." But, as Raw, Page, and Hodgson explain, the deal was far more complicated. The actual purchase, from an American company named King Resources, of a half interest in permits to explore twenty-two million acres of the Arctic, which the Fund of Funds made for $11 million in cash, was handled by John King, a Denver financier whose specialty was syndicating shares in oil wells (and in tax-avoidance ventures) for small investors buying on the installment plan. In the Arctic transaction, King, a close business associate of Cornfeld's, virtually acted for both sides. He was principal adviser to the Fund of Funds' Natural Resources Account and was also the head of King Resources. It was in 1969 that the Fund of Funds bought its half interest in the Arctic permits for $11 million from King's company, which had acquired all the permits in exchange for "work obligations." Then, early in January 1970, instead of selling a million acres of land for $14 an acre, as the *Times* and other publications reported, the Fund of Funds actually transferred 10 percent of its interest in the permits back to King Resources. The Fund of Funds received only $606,619 in cash for returning this fraction of its interest in the permits—a fraction for which it had paid $1,100,000—with the promise that it would receive $5,795,727 in six years' time. This obligation is not apt to be met, for King Resources got into severe financial difficulties shortly after the crisis in I.O.S. But even if the money were to be paid, the transfer would still be a far cry from the reported $14 million sale.

These bookkeeping transactions—for little cash ever changed hands—did, however, produce an enormous profit for I.O.S. Cornfeld, on the basis of his claim to have sold a portion of his "rights" to an outside interest for $14 an acre, estimated that the rest of his rights were now worth $156 million. Thus, though no trace of oil had been found, the Fund of Funds suddenly increased the gross value of what it called its Arctic holdings by $145 million. The increase, made just in time for a year-end statement, was of great value to I.O.S. and its management in several ways. To begin with, it allowed I.O.S., which was charging the fund a "performance fee" based on increases in the value of the fund, to take in an additional $9.7 million, based solely on the overnight growth of the value of these very frozen assets; thus, investors who had paid $11 million for some rather dubious "rights" now paid a $9.7 million fee for the paperwork involved in inflating the value of those rights. Furthermore, this fee made it appear that I.O.S. had realized a sizable profit in 1969, when in fact it had barely broken even. This illusion was particularly important because a large block of shares in I.O.S. had just been offered to the public. Finally, insiders who were aware that the permits had been overoptimistically evaluated could redeem their shares in the Fund of Funds at an artificially high price, because the fund, like all open-end mutual funds, agreed to redeem shares at their net-asset value. Less well-informed investors, of course, were at this time buying shares in the Fund of Funds at artificially high prices.

Eventually, as redemptions drained the cash and the other liquid assets out of the fund, the Arctic bubble burst. In August 1970 the Fund of Funds spun off its natural-resources holdings into a newly formed subsidiary, Global Natural Resources; consequently, the price of Fund of Funds shares was reduced, again overnight, from $18.49 a share to $7.44 a share. Fund of Funds shareholders received shares in the new company as compensation, but at the end of 1970 an I.O.S. reassessment declared that most of the Arctic acreage had "little present economic value," since much of it was "at water depths making development under presently available techniques impracticable."

At the time of the I.O.S. collapse, the *Times* described Cornfeld's career as "one of the great success stories of the postwar period." The explanation generally presented in the American press of how a social worker from Brooklyn managed to achieve control of a $2 billion pool of capital in less than fifteen years was that Cornfeld, after establishing himself in Paris, used, in *Newsweek's* words, "brash American sales techniques," and, in *Time's* terms, flouted tradition, thereby creating what *Business Week* called "a genuine revolution in finance." *Newsweek* noted back in 1964 that Cornfeld's "brilliant young executives (average age: 35) so far at least have kept all his projects on track." *Fortune,* in discussing Cornfeld's "American methods" in March 1968, published a full-page chart to demonstrate "the extraordinary number of ways in which Cornfeld has succeeded in using one kind of business to help another," explaining that "the administrative headquarters in Geneva, helped by systems-development teams in the Bahamas, coordinates the finances of the entire empire." The *Times* referred to Cornfeld as a "supersalesman."

Raw, Page, and Hodgson point out that Cornfeld began his overseas financial career, in 1955, by selling mutual funds to American servicemen in France and then to other expatriates with legitimate access to dollars and other hard currency. But after he had set up a mutual fund of his own, in 1960, the really substantial inflow of money, which turned into a flood in the mid-sixties, came not in dollars invested by Americans living abroad but in foreign currencies put up by citizens of countries that restricted the export of local capital. A citizen of one of these countries could, in effect, convert the local currency into dollars by buying mutual-fund shares that could be cashed in for dollars abroad. Such transactions constituted illegal flights of capital. In tracing the flow of money from "soft-currency" countries into I.O.S. (a process that, Raw, Page, and Hodgson note, was camouflaged "with all the elaborate secrecy of an espionage service," complete with "secret processing centers," "baffling code names," and numbered accounts), the authors of *Do You Sincerely Want to Be Rich?* estimate that "not less than $250 million of I.O.S.'s first $700 million came from Latin America," where sales of I.O.S. mutual funds for local currencies were in many cases illegal, and where a number of I.O.S. salesmen were eventually arrested. (Their commissions had evidently made the risks seem worthwhile.) In Italy, during the years 1965 through 1969, the authors report, "the lowest estimate any of the managers we talked to gave us for the volume of illegal business was $12 million a month." Remarkably high volumes were also reported from Spain, Portugal, Greece, and Iran, where such sales were largely illegal. A director of I.O.S. told the authors, "You must never forget that the company developed out of the illegal areas." All this suggests that Cornfeld was successful in drawing capital into his funds not primarily because he was some sort of "supersalesman" but simply because he was operating what amounted to a black market in currency.

In scrutinizing the financial statements of I.O.S. at the time it offered its stock to the public, in 1969, Raw, Page, and Hodgson found that it was "a company scarcely profitable, if at all, in terms of its rationally predictable income, which was from the sale and routine management of mutual funds," but, rather, was "a company whose profits were increasingly cobbled together from a series of on-off deals and speculations." Basically, the problem was that for I.O.S. the cost of selling its funds was somewhat greater than its share of the commissions, which were also being split among salesmen and an elaborate hierarchy of sales managers, and that the overhead of maintaining an overseas financial complex absorbed most of the routine fees for managing funds, which, in any case, are relatively low. In order to go on selling shares of I.O.S. funds to the public, the company had to show high earnings, and this necessity led to a number of extraordinary deals and ad hoc manipulations—such as the Arctic revaluation—which could not be sustained. What happened to the money that I.O.S. received from the sale of its own stock to the public? According to Raw, Page, and Hodgson, of a total of $52 million raised, some $8 million was quickly used to buy back I.O.S. stock from Cornfeld and other top executives who wanted to cash in, and the balance was used in price-support operations and the financing of various tax-avoidance schemes. As the liquid assets disappeared, a crisis was inevitable.

To a large extent, journalism is still essentially "criticism of the moment at the moment," as William James defined it, and perhaps reporters, operating under daily deadlines and within tight news budgets, cannot be expected to do more with a subject as labyrinthine as I.O.S. than present a day-to-day summary of charges and countercharges. A great many pertinent facts did come out in the press about I.O.S., including the year-end profit made by the revaluation of the Arctic "rights," and the company's difficulties with the S.E.C. The problem was not that information about I.O.S.'s most flagrant manipulations was lacking but that nearly all the information came out piecemeal, and in a context of colorful personal extravagance and technical mismanagement, so that an understanding of the organizing concept of malfeasance was usually obscured. It took a British team of writers working on a long-term project for a London Sunday newspaper—a type of paper that relies much more for circulation on feature exposés than its American counterparts do—to present a comprehensive report on I.O.S. and to suggest some of the serious questions that need to be raised about all financial institutions based "offshore," outside the purview of governmental regulations. These latter-day muckrakers have also raised some serious questions about the effectiveness of business reporting in the American press.

—"Do You Sincerely Want to Be Rich?"
The New Yorker, February 1971

HISTORY AS FICTION

In 1964, Jacqueline Kennedy and Robert F. Kennedy commissioned William Manchester, a journalist who had formerly edited *Current Events* and other junior high school publications, to write the official history of the assassination of President John F. Kennedy. Their subsequent event to edit the "history" provoked an outcry in the media which focused on the issue of the "freedom" of the press to report history.

Throughout the protracted controversy surrounding the publication of William Manchester's *The Death of a President* the press seemed preoccupied with a single issue: the suppression of history. Did the Kennedys have the right to "censor" a historical chronicle which might prove personally embarrassing or which might jeopardize their political aspirations? Could Manchester be legitimately held to a contract which, in effect, allowed the Kennedy family to decide what he might or might not write? Should Jacqueline Kennedy have had the prerogative to delete from the historical record material which she considered in "poor taste"? In short, could the "public's right to know" be abridged by the people closest to the tragedy of the assassination and most vulnerable to its effects?

In the midst of all this, however, the question which would seem to have had the most direct bearing on the dispute was seldom broached: Just what kind of history was the Manchester book? Of course, during the controversy the working press was hardly in a position to cope with this question. Both Manchester's publisher and *Look* (which had purchased the serialization rights for an unprecedented $655,000) treated the manuscript as if it were a top-secret document. Even if some reporter could have got hold of a copy, the job of evaluating the 1,200-page unfootnoted text would have posed an enormous problem. How could one test the soundness of a work based, according to its author, on over a thousand interviews which he had conducted as well as on confidential materials, such as the classified files of the Warren Commission, which were available to no other journalist?

In any case, there was scant reason to doubt that an authorized historian, working as long and as hard as Manchester had, would produce anything less than a complete and honest account. In terms of sheer quantity—"100 hours a week" for nearly three years, 360,000 words, 18 volumes of transcribed interviews, $655,000—it all appeared to add up to *the* definitive history of the assassination. Even when *Time,* in one of the more perceptive reviews to date, pointed to significant factual errors and other major flaws in the published version of the book, it still concluded that "there is no question that Manchester did an honest and herculean job."

Quite conveniently for Manchester, the issue at hand was not the soundness of the book but the attempted censorship. Thus, *New York Times* reporter John Corry could devote thirty thousand words to a memo-by-memo account of the Kennedy efforts to alter Manchester's text, without ever confronting the more substantive question of whether the original book was in fact valid as history.

What was at stake in his battle with the Kennedys, Manchester proclaimed sententiously in his *Look* apologia,* was "the integrity of a historical document." "No one," he declared, "has the right to distort the past; no fact, however disagreeable, may be expunged from the record." As evidence of the probity and merit of his work, Manchester quoted "encomiums" from three distinguished readers of the early manuscript. Evan Thomas, his editor at Harper & Row, called it "the finest book I've read in twenty years here." Arthur Schlesinger, Jr., who read the text at Manchester's own request, stated in a memorandum to the author: "I think this is a remarkable and a potentially great book." And Richard N. Goodwin, an adviser to the Kennedy family, described it, according to Manchester, as "a masterful achievement."

But these "encomiums" were not, as Manchester himself knew only too well, all that the three men had had to say about the manuscript.

*"Manchester's Own Story," *Look*, April 4, 1967.

On May 16, 1966, after having reread it, Evan Thomas wrote to Edwin O. Guthman and John Siegenthaler, who were then acting as Robert Kennedy's representatives, that he was "deeply disturbed by some of this. . . . It's almost as though Manchester had become so deeply involved in this tragic narrative that he could not resist turning it into a magic fairy tale." Schlesinger, in the same memorandum from which Manchester so proudly quoted, had gone on to warn that the portrait of Lyndon Johnson "too often acquires an exaggerated symbolism—so much so that some critics may write that the unconscious argument of the book is that Johnson killed Kennedy (that is, that Johnson is an expression of the forces of violence and irrationality which ran rampant through his native state and were responsible for the tragedy of Dallas)." For his part, Goodwin, in a public statement, commented that the original manuscript contained "horrifying and unjust implications" as well as fictional passages.

A magic fairy tale? A subliminal *MacBird?* An unreliable fiction? Manchester dismissed these charges as part of a Kennedy conspiracy to discredit his work. "A great many gifted men were staking their careers on an RFK administration," he explained. "Now, the pull of loyalty was irresistible; they flocked to the standard." But that easy explanation fails to resolve all one's doubts. To understand what in fact disturbed these privileged readers so much, one must return to the original manuscript which they had before them in the spring of 1966.

*　　　*　　　*

The title of that book—which I myself had the opportunity to read many months before the controversy—was not *The Death of a President* but *Death of Lancer*.* Far from being simply a detailed and objective chronicle of the assassination, it was a mythopoeic melodrama organized around the theme of the struggle for power between two men, John Kennedy and Lyndon Johnson. As will be seen, however, the characters bearing these names in *Death of Lancer* have at best a questionable relation to the real persons themselves.

The protagonist of *Death of Lancer* is Kennedy ("Lancer" being his Secret Service code name). He is portrayed as a princely young knight, who always "charged forward at full gallop, bugles bugling and lances at full tilt." The antagonist, Johnson, appears as "a different creature" altogether. According to Manchester, "Johnson wouldn't even charge into a bathroom."

Kennedy is everything that Johnson is not. There is "a magical quality" and sense of "high drama" about this "lithe young figure"; Johnson, on the other hand, has "a gaunt, hunted look" about him. Whereas Kennedy is "D'Artagnan," the patrician hero, Johnson is "Richelieu," the "crafty schemer." In fact, Manchester—whose own editor found the manuscript "gratuitously and tastelessly insulting to Johnson"—sees John-

---

*It should be noted that *Death of Lancer* was substantially revised *before* it was sent to *Look* and other magazines for bidding on serialization rights. The legal battle was concerned *only* with material offensive to Mrs. Kennedy that remained in *The Death of a President* even after this original editing.

son in *Death of Lancer* as a one-man menagerie: "an oyster who patiently converts bits of grit into salable pearls"; a "chameleon who constantly changes loyalties"; a "six-winged lion"; a "creature of the moment." In short, as one Dallas friend of the Kennedys is represented as warning, "Lyndon is poison."

For all the differences between them, the two men have a common ambition: both want to be President. Manchester points to events at the Democratic party convention in 1960 as the source of the bitter rivalry. In 1960 Johnson had tried to "wrest" the Presidential nomination from Kennedy, who, he writes, "had been smitten by Johnsonian partisans." In the original text, Manchester identifies Texas Governor John Connally as the leader of the Johnson forces, who "had spread rumors that Kennedy would not live out his first term because he was 'diseased.' " When this pernicious tactic failed, Johnson had to settle for the role of Vice-President and heir-apparent.

On the very first pages of *Death of Lancer,* the duel for power is gruesomely symbolized in a hunting scene in which a reluctant President Kennedy finds himself forced to kill a deer at the LBJ ranch. As an opening scene, this episode (which is less conspicuously placed in *The Death of a President*) has the effect, as Schlesinger noted in his memorandum, "of defining the book as a conflict between New England and Texas, decency and vulgarity, Kennedy and Johnson."

The drama then shifts forward three years in time. The dark prophecy made by "Johnsonian partisans" at the convention—that Kennedy would not live out his first term—now seems remote. Kennedy has become a magnificent President, "the darling of the population." As for Johnson, "three years of relative inactivity had sapped [his] vitality." He now looks "haggard" and "atrophied." Formerly "red-blooded," he is now "anemic." Even as a force in Texas politics, he has become "virtually impotent," and he is no longer an effective figure on Capitol Hill. Expecting him to help with Congress, Manchester observes, is now "like expecting an erection from a paramecium. It couldn't work. The creature had no member." In sum, Johnson is "a capon."

Such epithets, it should be pointed out, are used in *Death of Lancer* purposefully, for they are integral to the larger theme of usurpation which is implicitly developed in the book: the antagonist is impotent until the assassination and only then regains his virility.

As Kennedy rises to the height of his glory, Johnson sinks to his nadir. Even such prestige as he now has is "counterfeit"—created, according to Manchester, by "publicity stunts" (notably when he "whooped his way through a blizzard of ticker-tape" meant for astronaut John Glenn, thus offending Kennedy's "austere sense of propriety"). Moreover, Johnson's proneness to "tergiversation" causes further worries in the administration, and at the highest levels "private doubts about Johnson's ability to serve as President" are expressed.

Johnson's "relative insignificance" is "driven home to him every day." For example, he is in the habit of sneaking aboard the President's plane, and on three different occasions when Kennedy aides find him "poking around its cabins alone," they are "obliged to ask the visitor to leave." These and other such incidents (for which, incidentally, I have been able to find no actual evidence) are, of course, "mortifying to a man of his extreme sensitivity."

Even more distressing to Johnson are the rumors that he may be "dumped from the ticket" in 1964. According to *Death of Lancer,* "this was more than newspaper gossip. In Texas representatives of the National Committee were repeatedly cornered by Johnson and Connally men who would talk of nothing else, and in Houston, U.S. attorney Woodrow B. Seals, a Kennedy appointee, had told a confidant that LBJ was too deeply involved in the Bobby Baker scandal and that the Attorney General, who despised corruption, would undoubtedly urge his brother to find another Vice-President."* LBJ begins to pick up these "alarming blips" on his "radar screen." He perceives that he is "in real trouble."

But Johnson has no intention of letting himself be purged. "Determined to prove his popularity . . . still strong," he proposes that Kennedy attend "four Texas banquets" (the last to be held in Dallas). Although Manchester never fully explicates all the reasons for the "expedition" to Texas, he leaves no doubt that Johnson's self-interest is to be served by Kennedy's trip to

a phantasmal of fog-shrouded bogs inhabited by outrageous giants who swagger about brandishing spiked cudgels. These improbable monsters were the local

---

*Woodrow B. Seals was not in fact interviewed by Manchester. At best, then, Manchester reported a secondhand rumor.

panjandrums. . . . The Jinn lived in a state of constant anarchy, raiding one another's castles and swatting innocent vassals. They were political cannibals, and a naïve outsider venturing among them could be eaten alive.

In this "lawless kingdom" to which Kennedy is being brought, there is "a blazing feud between two of the greatest ogres, the roaring flames of which the President must first pass through and then quench." (In other words, Kennedy had to settle an intra-party squabble.)

As both a Catholic and a liberal, the President was "doubly condemned" in Texas. "Under frontier justice, there was only one thing to do with renegades who willfully took the side of the savages. You didn't gab about it, you didn't hedge, you didn't hesitate. You just killed him."

Omens, premonitions and signs appear as the drama builds to its inevitable climax. A few days before Kennedy's arrival in Dallas, Secret Service agent Forrest Sorrel rides over the motorcade route. Glancing up at the city's "phallic" skyline, he says to himself, *"I've killed deer closer than that."* The reader's mind is thus driven round full circle—both by the image and by Manchester's italics—to where the book began, the deer hunt at the LBJ ranch.

Meanwhile, back at the ranch itself, Lyndon Johnson is completing the preparations for Kennedy's visit. "He had done everything a Vice-President can do," Manchester notes with his customary irony of hindsight, "unless, of course, the President dies."

In their final meeting in the Rice Hotel in

Houston, Johnson and Kennedy have a heated argument, apparently having to do with the question of Johnson's veracity. And then Kennedy is murdered. To Manchester, the "shattering fact" in this original version is that "A Texas murder had made a Texan President." Over and over again, Manchester stresses this idea, even having Kenneth O'Donnell exclaim: "They did it. I always knew they'd do it. You couldn't expect anything else from them. They finally made it." Manchester adds: "He didn't specify who they were. It was unnecessary. They were Texans, Johnsonians. . . ."

Lyndon Johnson's reaction to the assassination in *Death of Lancer* is to throw out the "red herring" of a "Communist conspiracy," hoping by this gambit to divert attention from his native state's responsibility for the atrocity. "If he could have charged that the shots had been fired from an orbiting satellite, he might have done so." But the inescapable fact, Manchester obsessively reiterates, is "that the reign of one ended and the other began in the head of a Texas marksman."*

As Manchester tells it in *Death of Lancer,* Johnson rushes to the airport to take possession of Air Force One, a long-coveted symbol of dominion. On board, in one of the most bizarre episodes in the book, the new President and his party engage in a "vegetable soup saturnalia." In Manchester's myth the death of Lancer brings the en-

---

*Lee Harvey Oswald was not a native Texan. He was born and raised in New Orleans, resided in New York City and Minsk, and had moved to Dallas from New Orleans less than two months before the assassination.

forced impotence of the tanist to an end: "Now he was alive again." Having been "a capon," he is now suddenly "a full-fledged hypomanic at the height of his vitality." He becomes "an octopus, clutching bunches of black bananas," "the shrewd manipulator," "the crafty seducer with six nimble hands," "one of those gifted seducers who can persuade a woman to surrender her favors in the course of a long conversation confined to obscure words; no woman, even a lady, can discern his intentions until the critical moment."

To understand fully what Manchester is implying in those passages, one must turn to two other passages. The first concerns Kennedy's apprehensions about his Vice-President:

To grasp what the possibility of succession means to an occupant of the White House it is necessary to ponder the meaning of the Presidency itself—the legacy the second man stands to inherit. A husband can take out a fortune in life insurance without flinching. His attitude would alter sharply if he were told that the man next door would, in the event of his death, become father to his children and husband to his wife.

The other relevant passage is the last chapter, "Legend," where Manchester discusses the "King Must Die" myth. The crux of this myth is that the king is ritualistically murdered and the appointed successor takes his place not only as ruler but as the queen's consort as well. And, indeed, in pursuit of this theme, Manchester goes so far as to invent an encounter on the airplane between Mrs. Kennedy and the new President. She becomes "the first member of the Presidential party to dis-

cover that Air Force One had a new commander"
when she opens her bedroom door in the plane
and sees Lyndon Johnson "sprawled" across her
husband's bed.* Manchester even suggests that
Johnson had "carefully laid out" Mrs. Kennedy's
"white Austin clothes" because "[the] new President wanted her to look immaculate in the inaugu-
ral picture so that the public's memory of the
maculate scene on Elm Street would be blurred."

After this strange flight back to Washington,
the original manuscript is not very different from
the published version. There is the funeral, the
catharsis, and the apotheosis in which John
Kennedy takes his place with King Arthur, Ro-
land, Balder the beautiful, and Jeanne d'Arc.

To be sure, the foregoing précis is taken from
a 1,200-page manuscript, and certain prominent
themes may seem less mythic when viewed as part
of the entire tapestry rather than as isolated
threads. Nevertheless, these threads do indicate, I
think, that the criticisms of Messrs. Thomas,
Schlesinger and Goodwin were provoked by
something more substantial than Manchester was
later willing to concede. It is one thing to bandy
about high-sounding phrases like "the integrity of

*That this episode is fiction we know from virtually all the other
evidence. For example, Lawrence O'Brien, who accompanied Mrs.
Kennedy and the coffin to the airport, clearly specified the sequence
of events. First, the coffin was brought onto the plane. "Then,"
O'Brien testified, "I looked up, and the President and Mrs. Johnson
were at the corridor . . . [on the plane]." *Next,* "Mrs. Kennedy came
aboard and was seated in the rear compartment, and Mrs. Johnson
and the President went over to her" (Warren Commission testimony,
Volume VII, p. 470). Thus, Mrs. Kennedy did *not* first encounter
Johnson in her bedroom—a fact which is supported by the testimony
of Kenneth O'Donnell, President Johnson, Secret Service agent Ki-
vett and others.

a historical document" and the "public's right to
know," as Manchester did in *Look*. But to infuse
a narrative with mythopoeic elements (e.g., the
usurpation theme, complete with ritual hunts, sat-
urnalias, ogres, and omens); to transform the par-
ticipants in the event into grotesque caricatures
(e.g., the successive portraits of President Johnson
as a feckless capon, a mendacious chameleon, and
a crafty seducer); and to create fictitious episodes
for the purpose of heightening the melodrama
(e.g., the first meeting between Johnson and Mrs.
Kennedy on the plane) is to forfeit the claim to be
compiling a "historical document," The early
readers of *Death of Lancer* all evinced concern
over the same point: the author's uncertain grip on
reality. Clearly, they were justified in that concern. For as Evan Thomas later said in explaining
why Manchester had turned the story of John
Kennedy's death into a "magic fairy tale," Manchester had "become so emotionally involved that
he had no choice but to give way to his emotions."

The potentially explosive nature of *Death of
Lancer* derived, however, not from its embarrassing excesses, but from the ineluctable fact that it
had been commissioned by Robert Kennedy and
would appear under the auspices of the Kennedy
name. Once *Death of Lancer* had been read by
Robert Kennedy's representatives, publication
understandably became contingent on the deletion
of the fictional parts of the book.

Manchester—the same Manchester who
subsequently identified himself in *Look* as "I, the
zealous defender of the public's right to know"
and declared that "no fact, however disagreeable,

may be expunged from the record"—readily
agreed to such deletions in his eagerness to get "an
approved text." Indeed, he wrote Guthman and
Siegenthaler, the Kennedy liaisons, that all the
anti-Johnson material and other passages detrimental to the "national interest" and the "Presidency" (*including* factual material) should be cut.

With the author's full consent, then, the more
unseemly subthemes were filtered out of the book.
The denigrating portrait of Lyndon Johnson was
transfigured into an almost sympathetic one. The
blackest villains (Johnson's partisans) enjoyed a
last-minute reprieve and were finally tinted gray.
Death of Lancer became *The Death of a President.*

Much of what was cut out, however, had
formed the unifying principle of the book, so that
the revisions had the effect of weakening its liter-
ary impact. The notion that Johnson, the successor, was somehow responsible for the death of his
predecessor is what gave the original melodrama
much of its thrust and such structural coherence
as it had. The omens, premonitions, mysterious
deaths, and thanatopsic pageantry all contributed
to a developing myth which began with a "ritual"
stag hunt and ended with a solitary stranger
standing spellbound as he unfolds the blood-
stained garments worn by Jacqueline Kennedy on
the day of the assassination. Without the mythic
overview, many details appear in the final book as
free-floating absurdities.

Thus, with Johnson exonerated, certain key
episodes—the moments of confrontation between
"loyalists" and "realists," Johnson's usurpation of
Air Force One, the boycott of the new President's

oath by Kennedy aides, the first Cabinet meeting with its oppressive tension—are reduced to little more than a disconcerting play of manners; the final text at times reads like a courtesy book for the Presidential company, prescribing proper etiquette in the aftermath of an assassination. The revisions also worked to obscure the motivation of certain principal actors in the drama Manchester originally constructed. The "loyalists," for example—O'Donnell, Powers, McHugh, Mrs. Kennedy—whose behavior toward Johnson in *Death of Lancer* makes sense in terms of the myth, appear curiously irrational and foolish in their gestures of opposition to the well-meaning Lyndon Johnson of *The Death of a President.*

But tempering the book's inordinately anti-Johnson tone did not enhance its claims to accuracy, for Manchester seems to have been as willing to reverse facts as he was to make the requested thematic revisions. For instance, to absolve Johnson of responsibility for the tragedy, it was convenient to overlook his participation in the planning of the trip to Texas. The final version states only that Connally met with Kennedy at the Cortez Hotel in El Paso the previous spring and gave his consent; a few pages later, Manchester says that Johnson "had not been consulted about the desirability of the expedition." The truth is, however, that Johnson also attended the meeting at the Cortez Hotel where, according to Clifton Carter, a participant in the conference, "the original conversation concerning President Kennedy's trip to Texas occurred." Manchester was indeed, as he wrote Mrs. Kennedy, "becoming an expert with the eraser."

Yet there were also certain points having nothing to do with "the integrity of a historical document" or "the public's right to know" on which Manchester refused to yield an inch. An example is his private joke about Brigadier General Godfrey McHugh. Apparently because McHugh served as Kennedy's personal weather forecaster, Manchester decided to truncate the general's first name and refer to him as "God." If the Presidential party encountered inclement weather, after McHugh had promised blue skies, Manchester could wryly note that "God had blundered badly. It wasn't the first time, either." No one begrudges an author a warranted *jeu d'esprit.* But as Schlesinger specifically pointed out in his memorandum to Manchester, McHugh was never called "God." Even so, Manchester insisted on retaining the joke.

Nor did Manchester defer to Professor Schlesinger's counsel in matters of historical scholarship. Part of the tendentious theory that the whole city of Dallas shared responsibility for the assassination rested on the author's flat assertion that "Pioneer society demands total conformity." Schlesinger suggested that any such premise was seriously challenged by Frederick Jackson Turner's thesis that the frontier bred individualism and advised that "the matter is too complicated to be solved here." But the "Manchester thesis" won out in the published book.

Strangely enough, Manchester seems to have been most intransigent in dealing with details palpably irrelevant to the history of the assassination. One of these was a scene in which the Kennedy

children are told of their father's death while being
bathed by their nanny. When the editors attempted to remove this scene on the ground that
it appeared to be spurious and was, moreover,
tasteless, Manchester protested vigorously that it
was "the most important" episode in the book. "It
simply cannot be omitted, and I cannot imagine
altering it in any way. I cannot exaggerate my
conviction on this. Of course it is upsetting. I don't
have to be reminded of that. For personal reasons
it was the most difficult passage I have ever written, and I still have not recovered from it. But it
cannot go. I will take anything but that."* It was
his inexplicable obstinacy on irrelevant points like
this, and not so much anything pertaining to the
political history of his subject, which apparently
led in the end to Manchester's legal skirmish with
the Kennedy family.

But a more critical test of a historian's
probity than his ability to discriminate between
the relevant and the irrelevant is his way of coping
with material which tends to conflict with his major theses. Does he take such material into proper
account, even if that might entail revising or
reconstructing his prime argument, or does he
simply omit it or disingenuously attempt to dis-
count its significance?

One such problem arose for Manchester in
May of 1966 (after *Death of Lancer* had been
completed), when it was revealed that there was a
salient contradiction between the FBI Summary
Report and the Warren Report concerning the

*Letter to Evan Thomas, May 13, 1963.

results of the autopsy performed on President
Kennedy. The only evidence capable of resolving
this contradiction, the unexamined X-rays and
photographs of the autopsy, were at that time "un-
available." Until these pictures could be scrutinized, crucial questions about the assassination
would remain moot.

Manchester's original text contained no mention of these photographs, but as soon as he became aware of their importance, he requested permission from Robert Kennedy's office to look at
them. Subsequently, in August, he added the following note to a revised version of his book:

The issue is resolved by the X-rays and photographs
which were taken from every conceivable angle during
the autopsy on the President's body. This material is
widely believed to be in the hands of the Secret Service.
In fact, it is the property of Robert Kennedy, who
decided that it was too unsightly to be shown to the
public, or even to members of the Warren Commission
staff. However, this writer is in a position to comment
upon it. The X-rays show no entry wound "below the
shoulder," as argued by the graduate student. Admit-
tedly X-rays of active projectiles passing through soft
tissue are difficult to read. However, the photographs
support them in this case—and clearly reveal that the
wound was in the neck.

When asked about this footnote by Richard N.
Goodwin, who was then acting as a consultant on
the book, Manchester let it be understood that he
had personally studied both the X-rays and the
photographs of the autopsy. Yet, as Goodwin later
learned to his dismay, permission had never been
granted Manchester to examine the photographs.

When presented with this fact, Manchester admitted that he had actually never seen either the X-rays or photographs, but was reluctant to change the text which was then being rushed to publication by *Look*.

Finally, under editorial pressure, he inserted a statement in the final version to the effect that he had not personally seen the autopsy pictures, but had discussed them with three men, each a stranger to the others, who carried "special professional qualification" and who had examined the evidence. Each gave, according to Manchester, accounts "identical" to the one he had reported in his August footnote. Manchester did not name the mysterious strangers, explain their special qualifications, or give details of their accounts (such as the exact location of the wound in the neck and whether or not the X-rays indicated a path for the missile). It would seem, then, that Manchester attempted to resolve a difficult and perplexing historical problem, first, by the device of a misleading statement implying an authority for himself he did not in fact possess, and then, when checked in the subterfuge, by inserting a revision which was itself needlessly vague and mystifying. Even so, he had imperiously asserted in behalf of his own interpretation of the assassination that "the account in the text is correct, and any version which contradicts it is inaccurate and insupportable."

This sleight-of-hand technique is further evident in Manchester's handling of material that demonstrably contradicted other cherished assumptions. In the *Look* serialization, Manchester

erroneously said that the photographs taken of
Johnson's swearing-in aboard Air Force One did
not show "the presence of a single male Kennedy
aide"; and that during the ceremony Kenneth
O'Donnell was "pacing the corridor like a caged
tiger, his hands clapped over his ears as though to
block the oath." Both these assertions were
promptly refuted. The Boston *Globe* published
one of the photographs of the ceremony showing
O'Donnell standing next to Mrs. Kennedy while
Johnson was being inaugurated. And *Time* identified six Kennedy aides—O'Donnell, Powers,
O'Brien, Clifton, Dr. Burkely, and Colonel Swin-
dal—in the same series of photographs which the
author had claimed showed not a single male
Kennedy aide.

Much of the drama Manchester extracted
from the alleged feud between the Kennedy and
Johnson camps was based on this supposed boycott of Johnson's "anointment"; it became especially prominent after other dubious sources of
conflict described in *Death of Lancer* had been
edited out of the final text. In the Harper & Row
edition, which was published about a month after
the errors were discovered in the *Look* serialization, the word "major" was added to "male
Kennedy aides." But this change hardly rectified
the mistake: all the "major" aides on the plane
were present, except perhaps for Godfrey
McHugh.

It is, of course, possible that Manchester simply lacked the time to make the necessary emenda-
tions before the book went to press. However, in
the changes Manchester submitted for the second

edition of *The Death of a President,* he proposed to add only that O'Donnell was "cropped out" of "the official photograph" because he had a "ghastly" look on his face as Johnson took the oath. But this planned revision compounded, rather than corrected, the original error. For one thing, there was no single official photograph, and for another, O'Donnell was cropped out of some pictures because they were, of course, photographs of Johnson, and O'Donnell was standing at the extreme edge of the crowd. Moreover, although his proposed revision appears to take care of the erroneous placement of O'Donnell, Manchester persists in leaving the impression of a boycott of Kennedy aides at Johnson's inauguration. Thus, even when Manchester was aware of substantial mistakes in his report, he preferred to sidestep rather than correct them.

Another example of this tendency can be seen in Manchester's treatment of J. Edgar Hoover. In his final version, he chides Hoover for his failure to extend condolences to the Kennedy family, and for remaining "sphinxlike." Yet Hoover had in fact written letters of sympathy to Robert Kennedy and other members of the family. To take care of this error, Manchester proposed adding that *although* Hoover had written a letter of sympathy, he remained "sphinxlike." The conclusion persisted even when the facts it was based on had vanished.

There is, however, little point in cataloguing Manchester's errors. Even critics who found *The Death of a President* seriously flawed by the author's lack of historical detachment assumed that the errors they themselves discovered were merely isolated examples in a vast reservoir of accurate facts; and they held forth the hope that Manchester's research and diligence had at least produced a valuable source book for later historians. But one commentator, Walter Lippmann, cut straight to the core of the matter: ". . . in the mistakes I know about there is the same pattern: always the mistake is a fiction which intensifies the drama of the story." If this is so, then far too many of Manchester's facts must remain suspect. Unless the arduous process of sorting out his facts from his dramatic fictions—a process only begun with the revisions of *Death of Lancer*—is completed soon, passing his work on to future historians as a primary source would be to cheat posterity of *its* "right to know."

—"The Death of Lancer
to Death of a President"
Commentary, July 1967

THE MAKING OF
A DEMAGOGUE:
THE PROBLEM OF
MANIPULATION

On March 1, 1967, Jim Garrison, the ambitious district attorney of New Orleans, arrested Clay Shaw, a fifty-four-year-old businessman, and charged him with "participating in a conspiracy to murder John F. Kennedy." Two years later, when the case finally came to trial, Garrison failed to produce any evidence whatsoever to substantiate this charge, and Shaw was acquitted in less than one hour. In the interim, however, Garrison made himself a nationally recognized figure, and had a substantial effect on the climate of public opinion in America.

If the press has any doubts about me, if they think I'm politically ambitious, if they really think I'd charge somebody for some kind of personal gain, then they should raise the question. That's fine. Because I'll survive. . . . (Jim Garrison speaking before the Radio and Television News Association of Southern California, November 1967)

A demagogue can survive only so long as the mass media take him seriously enough to print his charges and give him exposure. The relation is not, however, entirely one-sided. The demagogue, free of any constraint of veracity, is always in a position to provide journalists with the kinds of exclusive stories and sensational charges which stimulate widespread interest—and circulation. The way in which Garrison's case developed, from the abrupt arrest and pretrial hearing of Clay Shaw to the constantly changing configuration of assassins and conspirators, is perhaps more closely connected to Garrison's struggle to obtain access to the news media than it is to his evidentiary investigation.

Life

Garrison decided to investigate the assassination of President Kennedy in November 1966 after he discussed the matter with Senator Russell Long on a plane flight to New York City. Shortly after he returned to New Orleans, the district attorney informed David Chandler, *Life*'s man in New Orleans, of his plans. He also suggested that *Life*, which had itself just called for a new inquiry into the assassination in a cover story entitled "A Matter of Reasonable Doubt" (November 25, 1966), might be interested in "a joint investigation." Chandler relayed the offer to the New York office, and Richard Billings, then an associate editor for special events, was promptly dispatched to New Orleans. On December 7, Garrison met with Billings and Chandler and offered to give *Life* reporters complete and exclusive access to his investigation. All he asked in return was that *Life* assist him in investigating matters outside his jurisdiction. Billings agreed to what he termed "an exchange of information," and for the next ten weeks *Life* photographers and reporters became an integral part of the district attorney's investigation: interviewing witnesses, photographing interrogation sessions, attending staff conferences, and preparing a major story on Garrison's prime suspect, David Ferrie. However, relations became somewhat troubled after Ferrie's sudden death in late February 1967 and, a week later, Garrison arrested a new suspect, Clay Shaw. Garrison later told me that he had been promised a cover story in *Life* if he made an arrest, and when it failed to materialize he realized that *Life* "had knuckled under to White House pressure." Billings categorically denied that any such commitment was ever made by representatives of *Life*. Chandler said that Garrison assumed from the amount of interest *Life* had manifested that an arrest would lead to a cover story, but no promises were ever made.

There were a number of reasons why *Life* never published the extensive story it had prepared on the Garrison investigation. Immediately after Shaw was arrested, Chandler, who had been present at the "brainstorming sessions" in which Garrison speculated that Clay Shaw might be the

elusive Clay Bertrand, informed senior editors at
Life that he now thought the entire investigation
might be a publicity stunt. Billings also had some
doubts after the arrest of Shaw: he had been present when Assistant District Attorney Sciambra
gave Garrison an oral report of Perry Raymond
Russo's story, and, at this time, it contained nothing about a "conspiracy" or about a "Bertrand"
who fitted the description of Shaw. The publication of James Phelan's devastating report on Garrison in the *Saturday Evening Post* was probably
the final straw. Garrison, apparently disappointed
over *Life*'s failure to publish, not only had granted
Phelan a long interview in Las Vegas, but had also
allowed him to examine the documents. Phelan
found a memorandum from Assistant Prosecutor
Sciambra which revealed that Russo's original
story was very different from the one he had told
in court—and although Garrison and Sciambra
publicly denied this, Billings was in a position to
know that it was true, and *Life* quickly lost interest after this in the Garrison affair.

Playboy

Garrison next sought exposure in *Playboy*, agree-
ing to allow the magazine to publish an extensive
interview about his investigation *before* the case
came to trial. The editor in charge of the project
estimated that the interview, which contained alle-
gations ranging from CIA involvement in the assassination to the arrival of Fascism in America,
represented "$1,605,000 worth of editorial space,"
although it is not clear whether he is referring to

the publicity which the interview would gain for *Playboy* or for Garrison. There is no reason to assume, however, that the decision to publish the interview was based primarily on mercenary considerations, for, in giving Garrison "the chance to present his side of the case" before the trial took place, *Playboy* was, after all, acting in the well-established tradition of American journalism which holds that every story has two sides—and that what is controversial is news. This concept of news does not necessarily require that an account, so long as it fairly represents one side of a story, be factually accurate. In recommending the interview for publication, one senior editor thus wrote:

Garrison comes off as sincere, eloquent, even brilliant. *But even if he were a nut*—and I don't think it's possible for anyone to read this and come away with that conclusion—I would still want to run this, just because it is the first complete reconstruction of the assassination events as seen through Garrison's eyes. At worst, if Garrison is totally repudiated (in light of the facts he presents this seems highly unlikely), we have an interview in the Shelton-Rockwell genre. At best, if he is vindicated, then we perform a genuine public service, almost in the Pulitzer prize category. [Italics in the original memorandum.]

A second editor's evaluation ran along similar lines:

Garrison is revealed as an intelligent, hearty, and ballsy guy—certainly not a kook—with a credible case, even if he turns out wrong. He indicts everyone from the CIA, to Warren's Commission, to NBC (he gets a bit gratuitous there and dissipates his venom), and he probably is somewhat paranoid, but I think anyone would be who was conducting a non-Establishment investigation into the assassination.

In a memorandum to Hugh M. Hefner, the publisher, Murray Fisher, a senior editor, summed up the reasons for publishing the interview:

Even if he's wrong (which is possible), even if he's insincere (which I doubt), even if the accusations about his impropriety are true (which seems not to be the case), Shaw is still going to go to trial in October [1967] and the interview (coming out two or three weeks before it begins) will be very big news.

Since the interview would be "big news" whether Garrison was right or wrong, there was little incentive to check out the factual accuracy of the piece before publication. (Almost all of Garrison's references to the testimony in the Warren Commission's volumes, which for the most part could have been checked without a great deal of effort, were either incorrect or misleading. For example, in purporting to quote from a Supplementary Investigation Report which appeared in Volume XIX of the Warren Commission's testimony, Garrison simply altered the words in the text from "I advised him" to "I was advised" to make his point.) Despite the prediction of A.C. Spectorsky, the associate publisher, that the interview would lead to twenty-four libel suits, it was rushed to publication in September to anticipate a trial that did not immediately materialize. And although *Playboy* may not have realized the expected $1,605,000 in free publicity, Garrison did his share by appearing on radio and television shows in New York and California in conjunction with the publication of the interview. In *Playboy,* the New Orleans district attorney found (as he put it in one of the television appearances) "an opportunity to try and communicate some of the issues in the case" to a national audience.

The Anti-Establishment Press

Moreover, Garrison found allies, eager to proselytize on his behalf, among dissident political writers who consider themselves part of what they call "the anti-Establishment press." His charge that there was a conspiracy between government and the mass media to conceal the truth from the people accords perfectly, after all, with what such journals see as their raison d'être. It is therefore hardly surprising to find his speeches printed verbatim in such papers as the Los Angeles *Free Press,* and to find his portrait on the cover of *Ramparts,* with the words:

Who appointed Ramsey Clark, who has done his best to torpedo the investigation of the case? Who controls the CIA? Who controls the FBI? Who controls the Archives where this evidence is locked up for so long that it is unlikely that there is anybody in this room who will be alive when it is released? This is really your property and the property of the people of this country. Who has the arrogance and the brass to prevent the people from seeing that evidence? Who indeed? The one man who has profited most from the assassination—your friendly President, Lyndon Johnson!

Garrison thus finally obtained the cover story that *Life,* despite his efforts, had denied him.

Anti-establishmentarianism tends to make strange bedfellows. Among Garrison's most ardent supporters was the *Councilor,* the bimonthly official journal of the Citizens' Council of Louisiana, which claims a circulation of some two hundred and sixty thousand, and which actively campaigns against Communism, the suppression of news by the mass media (supposedly controlled by Zionist interests), race mongrelization (a plot aided by the CIA and the Rothschilds), and the insidious intrusion of federal authority into the sacred domain of states' rights. That Garrison had been "fought by Sterns, Newhouse papers, and Agnes Meyer" (i.e., the NBC affiliate in New Orleans, WDSU-TV; the *Times-Picayune* and *States-Item;* and the *Washington Post* and *Newsweek*) was for the *Councilor* sufficient reason to lend Garrison its enthusiastic support. The logic of *Ramparts* has not been significantly different; William Turner concluded one of his articles on Garrison in the magazine by saying that the anti-Garrison tactics of NBC, *Newsweek* and the daily press "smack of desperation—and indicate that there is much to hide." The *Councilor* went along with most of the details of the plot theory outlined in *Ramparts,* differing only in its belief that it was "the left wing of the CIA," not the right wing, and that New York Communists, rather than right-wing extremists, were behind the conspiracy. (Perry Russo told the *Councilor* in an exclusive interview that David Ferrie was really a "Marxist" and follower of Che Guevara.)

The New York Review

Garrison's cause also found champions in more
highly respected journals that pride themselves on
their intellectual credentials—notably the *New
York Review of Books,* which rejected the Warren
Commission's conclusions because the commission's investigation was defective and embraced
Garrison's investigation despite its far more glar-
ing defects. Professor Richard Popkin, in a
lengthy defense of Garrison's investigation in the
New York Review, argues that Garrison should be
given a "fair hearing" in court, and not have his
case "prejudged" by the press. He claims that
while Garrison has "studiously avoided any discussion of Shaw and the specific evidence against
him," the press has interviewed "potential witnesses," evaluated the evidence, made "charges
against the District Attorney and his office . . . in
effect, trying the case out of court." The "wave of
attacks in the press and TV" against Garrison,
Popkin contends, "surely prejudices a fair trial."
He concludes that no investigation of Garrison is
necessary, for "if the evidence is as contrived and
cockeyed as the press and TV allege, they should
expect that twelve jurors along with the judge will
see through it." It is true that the right of a defendant not to be prejudged is a fundamental principle
of jurisprudence. And pretrial publicity, by pre-
judicing public opinion, can certainly deny the
defendant his right to a fair hearing. Jim Garrison,
however, is *not* the defendant. Clay Shaw was!
The rights of the defendant have been established

precisely to counterbalance the powers of the state. Popkin's plea that the press suspend scrutiny and criticism of Garrison's methods would, if it were taken to heart, undermine a defendant's legitimate protection against the possibility of a prosecutor's using his power and resources to fabricate evidence and intimidate witnesses. Moreover, Popkin's contention that Garrison "studiously avoided" discussing the evidence seems disingenuous, at best. The fact is that an interview that Popkin had with Perry Russo was arranged by the district attorney himself. It was Garrison, too, who told reporters that he had found Jack Ruby's coded telephone number in both Shaw's and Oswald's address books, and repeated the allegation on television and to newspaper reporters even after it was shown to be false. It was Garrison who stated in the *National Observer,* "There is no way that Clay Shaw can get an acquittal." It was Garrison who allowed Mark Lane and William Turner to photostat evidence in his files. And it was Garrison who, in his *Playboy* interview on his subsequent coast-to-coast tour, made numerous references either to evidence in the Shaw case or to Shaw himself (including the demonstrable falsehood that Shaw was with President Kennedy "on an airplane flight in 1963"). Indeed, Garrison went on about the case in speeches, radio talk shows, television programs, press conferences and interviews almost without pause. Of course, most of the evidence Garrison discussed is spurious, but surely that makes it all the more imperative for the press not to waive its responsibility for examining it closely.

Popkin's way of dismissing the charges leveled against Garrison is similarly cavalier. He
chides *The New York Times* for accepting at face
value, and printing on its front page, the allega-
tions made against Garrison by the convicted bur-
glar John Cancler; Popkin points out that when
the grand jury later questioned Cancler about the
accusations, he invoked the Fifth Amendment.
The fact that Cancler exercised his Constitutional
right to protect himself against self-incrimination,
Popkin concludes, affects the "credibility" of his
charges. Yet, does this necessarily follow? Cancler
had charged that his fellow prisoner, Vernon
Bundy, confided to him that he was going to give
perjured testimony at Clay Shaw's preliminary
hearing, testimony that would inculpate Shaw. If
this is true, Cancler was an accessory before the
fact in the perjury, and might indeed have in-
criminated himself by admitting this to the grand
jury. Besides, the mere fact that Cancler took the
Fifth Amendment, though it may have signaled a
want of courage on his part, surely cannot be said
to affect in itself the man's credibility (although
there were those among the followers of the late
Senator Joe McCarthy who insisted that it did).

Popkin's notion that there is no need for the
press to scrutinize Garrison's techniques for recruiting witnesses and assembling evidence, because if the evidence is contrived a judge and jury
will see through it and "destroy Garrison at the
trial," shows an unusual degree of confidence in
the legal process. While it is true that a judge and
ry can detect contradictions in testimony and
r incongruous evidence, there is no certainty

at all that they can uncover perjury that has been systematically arranged for, with one perjurer corroborating another's testimony, or that they can recognize artfully fabricated "facts" purposely designed to fit into the pattern of evidence. Exposure of such systematic fraud would, in fact, depend on an outside investigation of the prosecutor's means and methods. Gene Roberts, of *The New York Times,* and Walter Sheridan, of NBC, have stated that in separate inquiries they discovered at least six witnesses who said that they had been offered bribes, blackmailed, or otherwise coerced by Garrison's representatives. All were, in one way or another, vulnerable people. William Gurvich said that while he was working for Garrison he saw the way the powers of a district attorney's office could be used "to intimidate and coerce witnesses." Popkin intimates that Sheridan and Gurvich may have had some ulterior motive in revealing information about Garrison's mode of operation. One can, as the British philosopher A. J. Ayer points out, always sustain one's beliefs in the face of apparently hostile evidence if one is prepared to make the necessary ad hoc assumptions, and in this case supporters of Garrison seem all too ready to assume that everyone who criticizes Garrison's conduct is part of a plot to conceal the truth. But such rationalization explains nothing. During the time I studied Garrison's investigation and had access to his office, the only evidence I saw or heard about that could connect Clay Shaw with the assassination was fraudulent—some devised by Garrison himself and some cynically culled from criminals or the emotionally unstable. To fail to report this information so that Garrison might have a "fair hearing" in court could preclude the possibility of the defendant's ever receiving *his* fair hearing in court.

To see the issue of the assassination as of such overwhelming importance that the juridical rights of the defendant may be neglected, the Constitutional rights of witnesses disdained, the scrutiny and criticism of the press suspended, and the traditional methods of the state's prosecution ignored is to accept a curious sort of situational ethics. It is to say that in the search for facts the means can be disregarded if the ends—the facts—are of enough consequence. Fred Powledge, writing in the *New Republic,* suggests the dilemma: "I had the irrational feeling that he [Garrison] was on to something. I had the equally startling feeling that it did not really matter if Garrison were paranoid, opportunistic, flamboyant, or if his witnesses were not candidates for *The Defenders.* Was he *right?* But can the process of establishing the truth ever be separated from its end product—the truth? Facts must be selected, interpreted, and arranged in the context provided by other information before they take on meaning. Factual evidence can be established as truth, as Hannah Arendt points out, only "through testimony by eyewitnesses— notoriously unreliable—and by records, documents, and monuments, all of which can be suspected as forgeries." If one has reason to doubt the process by which the "facts" have been ascertained or confirmed, how can one ever be certain that they bear any relation to the truth, or even that the "facts" themselves are not outright fabrications? For data can be accepted as factual truth if, and only if, the probity of the investigator is also accepted. A demagogue who demonstrates a willingness to alter elements of a story when it serves his purpose may temporarily excite public opinion, but he can never establish his version of the event as the truth.

The principal consideration operating to restrain a duly elected district attorney from making indiscriminate arrests and charges—aside from normal ethical considerations—is fear of exposure by the press if supporting proof should not be forthcoming. Yet, despite some cogent evidence of malfeasance on Garrison's part reported by a number of journalists, public-opinion polls indicated that there was actually a substantial increase in the number of people, not only in Louisiana but throughout the country, who shared Garrison's belief in a conspiracy. If in fact his case was based on little more than wild rumors and the unsubstantiated testimony of unstable witnesses, why was the press so ineffective in checking Garrison? In his study of the late Senator Joseph R. McCarthy, Richard H. Rovere demonstrates how a certain kind of demagogue, when he is assailed by the press, can turn the hostile criticism to his own advantage. Such a demagogue builds his political base on the systematic exploitation of inchoate fears, and sets about organizing a popular flight from reality. To him, even the most vocal censure, however adverse its ostensible effect, represents useful publicity, for the more rigorously he is assaulted by the press, the more prominently he figures in the popular imagination. A false charge has to be repeated if it is to be refuted, and if the charge happens to be more appealing than the truth, it is entirely possible that it, rather than its refutation, will win general credence. This is especially likely to occur if the demagogue's charge offers a more or less plausible explanation of disturbing events, and if its refutation depends on the word of government officials, since the people most apt to accept conspiratorial interpretations of history are those who are most suspicious of both complexity and authority. As Rovere points out with regard to McCarthy, the demagogue soon learns that "the penalties for a really audacious mendacity are not as severe as the average politician fears them to be, that, in fact, there may be no penalties at all, but only profit."

In a sense, the man who exploits popular fears builds his reputation on the prestige of his adversaries. The more impressive the list of detractors he can cite, the more important his charges appear to be. "Why are they trying to destroy me?" the demagogue asks. But the surest benefits he derives from being publicly criticized are the "right to reply"—a right that is greatly enhanced by the demands of day-to-day reporting, which cause the press to focus more directly on the individual under attack than on the general issue at stake—and the results of the ethic of "objective reporting"—which in practice usually means no more than that the individual criticized gets the last word in the news stories. If the demagogue is challenged on radio or television, he can demand equal time to respond. And, of course, his reply need not restrict itself to a defense of his original position. Indeed, to obfuscate the issue further and mitigate the attack on him, the demagogue may strike out in an altogether different direction. For he is, typically, concerned not with substantive issues but with ways of manipulating the emotions of the electorate.

One way Garrison responded to attacks made on his thesis that there was a conspiracy to kill President Kennedy was by talking about a second conspiracy that grew out of the first one—a conspiracy of secrecy dedicated to concealing the truth about the assassination. As in a speech he gave in December 1967 in New Mexico entitled "The Rise of the Fourth, or How to Conceal the Truth about an Assassination Without Really Trying," Garrison often seemed more deeply preoccupied with exposing an insidious misprision of felony on the part of federal authorities than with establishing the fact of the assassination itself. To be sure, such an obsessional concern with governmental suppression is not a new phenomenon, nor is it limited to the assassination issue. The political-sociologist Edward Shils has pointed to a highly suggestive link between the generalized fear of secrecy and the Populist tradition in America. In his book *The Torment of Secrecy,* he argues that a repugnance toward secrecy is so deeply ingrained in American political life that even in matters involving national security, secrecy is tolerated only as a necessary evil. To exploit this fear of secrecy, a truly Machiavellian politician could be expected to portray himself as engaged in a life-and-death struggle to wrest secrets from some powerful elite that controls the government and the news media, and to interpret all criticism leveled against him as part of a plot to conceal the dark truth from the populace.

Attack and Counterattack:
Saturday Evening Post

The first full-scale criticism of Garrison came in the last week of April 1967, in the *Saturday Evening Post,* when, in his article entitled "Rush to Judgment in New Orleans," James Phelan revealed that the crucial part of Perry Raymond Russo's testimony—the section incriminating Clay Shaw—was contradicted by a statement Russo had made earlier to Assistant District Attorney Sciambra. The day Phelan's story appeared, a bold headline in the *New Orleans States-Item* announced, MOUNTING EVIDENCE LINKS CIA TO "PLOT" PROBE. The article under this head, which implied that the CIA was attempting to block Garrison's efforts because former agents were involved in the conspiracy, had been prepared by several *States-Item* reporters, including Hoke May and Ross Yockey, who reportedly had a close working relationship with the Garrison investigation. Whether by design or by accident, the charges against the CIA effectively overshadowed the Phelan story, at least in New Orleans.

Newsweek and the CIA

Two weeks later, in an article written by Hugh Aynesworth, *Newsweek* reported that a witness had been offered a $3,000 bribe to implicate Clay Shaw in the conspiracy. The offer had been secretly tape-recorded by the witness's lawyer. Although the tape left it unclear whether the money was to be in payment for true information or false, it was damaging under any circumstances. (At one point, Garrison's representative said, "We can change the story around.") When Garrison learned of the impending *Newsweek* disclosure, he prepared a memorandum on CIA participation in the assassination; this document promptly found its way into the hands of Yockey and May, who wrote it up in an exclusive story in the *States-Item*. Upon being asked about the *Newsweek* charges, Garrison answered by confirming the *States-Item* report on the CIA. "The federal agents who concealed vital knowledge regarding President Kennedy's assassination, and their superiors who are now engaged in a dedicated effort to discredit and obstruct the gathering of evidence, are guilty of being accessories after the fact to one of the cruelest murders in our history," he declared, and he went on to warn that "the arrogant totalitarian efforts of these federal agencies to obstruct the discovery of truth is a matter which I intend to bring to light." An article in *The New York Times* the following day, May 16, attested to Garrison's success in blurring these charges with his own: although the *Times* article focused on the *Newsweek* report, the headline read: GARRISON CHARGES CIA AND FBI CONCEAL EVIDENCE ON OSWALD.

Garrison continued his offensive by issuing a subpoena for Richard Helms, the director of the Central Intelligence Agency, demanding that

Helms produce a photograph showing Oswald in the company of a CIA agent in Mexico. Subsequently, it was made plain that Garrison had no reason to believe that a photograph showing Oswald with a CIA agent had ever existed, but Garrison's subpoena drew national coverage and tended to dilute further the effect of the *Newsweek* story. It is worth noting that before Garrison subpoenaed the director of the CIA he had considered another move—arresting Regis Kennedy, an FBI agent in New Orleans who had taken part in the government's investigation of the assassination. Garrison explained to his chief investigator, William Gurvich, that although the agent would deny the charge, the denial would only add to the effect of criminally charging an FBI agent. But Garrison had second thoughts about attacking the FBI and, according to Gurvich, chose the CIA because, as Garrison himself put it, "they can't afford to answer."

Later, in May, when Garrison's claim that the notation of a Dallas post-office box in Clay Shaw's address book was actually Ruby's encoded telephone number was debunked by Lee Odom, the owner of the box, Garrison countered by charging that Oswald's address book contained an encoded version of the local CIA telephone number in New Orleans (though he later had to admit that the code was "subjective"). Then, further obscuring questions arising from his dubious interpretation of the "telephone codes," Garrison stated that both Oswald and Ruby had been CIA agents, and asserted on a local television show a few days later that the CIA knew the identity of the other assassins, but, he said, "We can't find out their names with the CIA keeping its vaults locked."

NBC and "Thought Control"

On the evening of June 19, 1967, NBC devoted an hour to a critical examination of Garrison's investigation entitled "The JFK Conspiracy: The Case of Jim Garrison." The first part of the program dealt with Russo's allegation that he had seen Oswald, Shaw, and Ferrie plotting the assassination at a party in Ferrie's apartment in September 1963. The NBC reporters demonstrated that at least one other person present at the party had not seen Shaw or Oswald there, and that Ferrie's bearded roommate, who Russo claimed was Oswald, had been identified by other people at the party as James Lewallen. The program then concentrated on Garrison's investigative methods, and a parade of witnesses was presented to allege that Garrison's representatives had attempted to bribe or intimidate them. In addition, NBC revealed that both of Garrison's key witnesses, Russo and Vernon Bundy, had failed lie-detector tests before testifying at the preliminary hearing. Frank McGee, the NBC anchorman, concluded, "The case he has built against Clay Shaw is based on testimony that did not pass a lie-detector test Garrison ordered—and Garrison knew it." The lie-detector evidence that NBC used to cap its case against Garrison was almost certainly the weakest part of that case. Yet the fact that NBC found it necessary to conclude its program with a concise statement of evidence established by the familiar and easily understood lie detector suggests a problem the mass media, and especially television, have in demonstrating a complex truth to their audience. Although the lie detector carries a certain authority in the popular imagination, and appears to give an unambiguous answer—the man is either lying or telling the truth—it is in fact merely a device for measuring the emotional stress that a witness is undergoing while he is being questioned. Such stress may indicate nervousness over deception, or it may indicate any of a number of other emotional responses. Since there is no objective way of differentiating among these responses, FBI Director J. Edgar Hoover had advised the Warren Commission in a memorandum that lie-detector tests were unreliable and of dubious value. NBC had assembled a good deal of cogent, if complex, evidence to show that Russo's allegation was untrue. But the effort to resolve for its mass audience the difficult issue it had so painstakingly presented by resorting to a simple and readily comprehensible indictment, based on evidence drawn from a source as dubious as lie-detector tests, left the program's conclusions open to serious criticism.*

Garrison, however, did not bother with serious criticism of the program's content; instead, he launched his counterattack by denouncing NBC as a party to an "Establishment" conspiracy to destroy him. "All of the screaming and hollering now being heard is evidence that we have caught

---

*NBC was not alone in employing lie detectors. *Newsweek*, the Chicago *Tribune*, and the Hearst Headline Service also used them to demonstrate that Garrison's case was based on untruths.

a very large fish," he proclaimed the morning after the NBC show. "It is obvious that there are elements in Washington, D.C., which are desperate because we are in the process of uncovering their hoax." To account for NBC's interest in his investigation, he told an interviewer that the network "is owned by Radio Corporation of America, one of the top ten defense contractors in the country." (It is actually twenty-seventh, according to the Department of Defense.) Garrison added, "All of these ladies of the evening are very much alike— the preferred customer is the one with the big bankroll and any position he suggests is eagerly assumed." Moreover, Garrison implied that the program had been secretly financed by the CIA.

Garrison wrote to the Federal Communications Commission to demand equal time, and NBC granted him a half-hour of prime evening time on July 15, 1967, to reply to the charges. Once on the air, however, he said, "I am not even going to bother to dignify the foolishness which *Newsweek* and NBC and some of the other news agencies have tried to make you believe about my office," and went on to denounce the media for manipulating the news and practicing "thought control." After giving five specific examples of "suppressed news," he presented his familiar argument that the attacks on his case attested to its validity: ". . . if our investigation was as haywire as they would like to have you think, then you would not see such a coordinated barrage coming from the news centers in the East." And he concluded: ". . . as long as I am alive, no one is going to stop me from seeing that you obtain the full truth, and nothing less than the full truth, and no fairy tales." Garrison had an audience of some twenty million, and for that, he said in his *Playboy* interview, he was "singularly grateful to Walter Sheridan," one of those who had prepared the NBC critique of his case.

Garrison's gratitude was less than total. Not long after the NBC program, he issued warrants for the arrest of Sheridan and also Richard Townley, who had assisted in the preparation of the show, charging them with attempted bribery. Specifically, Garrison alleged that they had offered Perry Russo a free trip to California.* But if this offer technically constituted an act of bribery, Garrison himself had taken considerable pains to bait the trap. He told me himself that he had directed Russo to speak to the reporters over a monitored phone and inquire what protection they could offer him if he were to change his testimony. The purpose was, as he put it, "to give NBC enough rope to hang itself." In his public statement on the matter, Garrison charged that the NBC program "will probably stand for many years to come as a symbol of the length to which some powerful outside interests are willing to go in order to interfere with state government." (The cases were subsequently dismissed.)

CBS and the "Establishment"

Shortly after Garrison's skirmish with NBC, William Gurvich resigned as one of his chief inves-

---

*Both Sheridan and Townley unequivocally denied the charges. Sheridan told me that it was Russo himself who suggested that NBC pay his expenses to California.

tigators, after telling the late Senator Robert F. Kennedy that there was no basis in fact and no material evidence in Garrison's case. Gurvich then appeared on the CBS-TV "News Inquiry" into the assassination and said he had resigned because "I saw no reason for the investigation. . . . The truth, as I see it, is that Mr. Shaw should never have been arrested." Gurvich's private-detective agency had conducted most of the lie-detector tests that Garrison had ordered, and at the time of his resignation Gurvich had in his possession a master file of the principal evidence in the case. This defection not only made for embarrassing headlines but opened up the possibility that Garrison's fund of confidential information—or his lack of such a fund—would be made public. In a statement to the press, Garrison described Gurvich's resignation as "the latest move from the Eastern headquarters of the Establishment to attempt to discredit our investigation." It was all part of a coordinated plot against him. In another press release, he said, "All they are doing is proving two things: first, that we were correct when we uncovered the involvement of the Central Intelligence Agency in the assassination; second, that there is something very wrong today with our government in Washington, D.C., inasmuch as it is willing to use massive economic power to conceal the truth from the people. Later, in his *Playboy* interview, Garrison implied that Gurvich had been a CIA infiltrator from the start. He also charged Gurvich with petty larceny, claiming the file that he had was worth nineteen dollars. And, for good measure, he charged on the ABC "Page One" television show that Senator Robert

Kennedy, whom Gurvich had earlier been in touch with, was "without any question of a doubt . . . interfering with the investigation of the murder of his brother" and was making "a real effort to stop it."

Pseudo-Attacks: Earl Warren and Lyndon B. Johnson

After it had become quite clear that criticism of Garrison's case could be used to generate a specter of conspiracy, Garrison took the logical next step and started creating pseudo-attacks on himself. When reporters in Tokyo asked Chief Justice Earl Warren his opinion of the Garrison investigation, he replied, "I want to skirt this very carefully, because the case could someday come before the Supreme Court." Pressed as to whether Garrison possessed any evidence that might contradict the findings of the commission he had headed, the Chief Justice answered, "I've heard that he claims to have such information, but I haven't seen any." Garrison immediately characterized this "new counter-attack" as "heavy artillery whistling in from Tokyo," and said in a press release, "It is a little disconcerting to find the Chief Justice of the United States on his hands and knees trying to tie some sticks of dynamite to the case. However, the Chief Justice is a practical man and I expect he knows what he is doing. . . . The last time he was called into action to perform a service was when the President of the United States was assassinated by men who had been connected with the Central Intelligence Agency." Garrison predicted a new broadside from the federal authorities: "Judging from the careful co-ordination which the Establishment showed in its last offensive against the case, it is safe to expect that other elements of the federal government and national press will now follow up with a new effort to discredit the case and the prosecution."

Another example of Garrison's technique involved Gordon Novel, a New Orleans electronics expert, who had told him about Ferrie's participation in a "pickup" of munitions from Schlumberger Well Surveying company, in Houma, Louisiana. Novel rapidly advanced from advising Garrison on anti-eavesdropping techniques, the business that had first brought him to Garrison's attention, to becoming a witness against Ferrie and, at least in Garrison's mind, an "investigator." Then, according to one account, Garrison was told that his investigator had been furnishing information to NBC reporters, and Novel was subpoenaed to appear before a grand jury. Instead of appearing, Novel left the state and went to Ohio. Garrison filed burglary charges against Novel, alleging that he had participated in the conspiracy to steal arms from the Schlumberger company, and he was arrested in Ohio. After some initial reluctance, Ohio Governor James Rhodes finally agreed to extradite Novel to Louisiana if Garrison would complete the papers within sixty days. Garrison, however, did not take the necessary steps. As the deadline approached,

Assistant District Attorney Alcock asked if he should return the papers to Ohio, and Garrison told him not to bother. After Garrison failed to reply to phone calls and telegrams from Ohio authorities inquiring about his intentions in the Novel case, and after the sixty-day period had elapsed, Judge William T. Gillie dismissed the extradition case against Novel. And yet in the *Playboy* interview, Garrison insisted, "The reason we were unable to obtain Novel's extradition from Ohio . . . is that there are powerful forces in Washington who find it imperative to conceal from the American public the truth about the assassination." He went on to indicate that Novel was now a material witness in his case and, according to attorneys for Novel, implied that his former "investigator" was somehow connected with the conspiracy. (Novel filed suit against Garrison and *Playboy* for $10 million in punitive and compensatory damages.) And in a speech to the Radio and Television News Association of Southern California, in Los Angeles, Garrison cited his failure to obtain Novel's extradition as evidence that President Johnson was putting pressure on local officials to secrete witnesses from him. He went on to accuse President Johnson of preventing "the people in this country from seeing the evidence," and asserted, with the logic of *cui bono,* ". . . the fact that he has profited from the assassination most, more than any other man, makes it imperative that he see that the evidence is released, so that we can know that he is not involved. . . ."

The New Yorker

When part of this essay was first published in *The New Yorker* in July 1968, Garrison responded in his customary style. Calling a press conference, the district attorney announced that an "intelligence agency of a foreign country . . . successfully penetrated the assassination operation," and that the "detailed information" he had received from this unnamed intelligence agency had "corroborated" statements he had previously made that President Kennedy was assassinated "by elements of the Central Intelligence Agency." He frankly admitted, according to *Time*, that the timing of the disclosure of the foreign assassination study was "designed to rebut" the charges in the *New Yorker* article (which he said was part of a "CIA-inspired campaign" to discredit his investigation). The "intelligence study" that Garrison referred to turned out to be nothing more than a pseudonymous manuscript entitled "The Plot" that had been sent to him three months earlier, after the *New York Review of Books* had rejected it. Garrison deduced that the manuscript "must have been written by a foreign intelligence agency, and probably the KGB" (the Russian counterpart of the CIA) because it contained "inside information" about the assassination. Actually, a good deal of the "inside information" that Garrison referred to had been, I found, previously published in William Manchester's *Death of a President* and in Garrison's own *Playboy*

interview. Garrison referred the manuscript to
Ramparts, whose editor also decided not to
publish it, after it was learned that the author
was merely a dissident European writer and not
a "foreign intelligence agency." Yet Garrison's
deployment of this manuscript was at least tac-
tically effective: the headlines of the New Orleans *Times-Picayune* on July 12, the day *The
New Yorker* appeared in New Orleans, read:
FOREIGN GROUP HAS FACTS—D.A., CIA ROLE
IN JFK DEATH CONFIRMED, HE SAYS.

POLITICAL TRIALS: THE PROBLEM OF COURT REPORTING

To what extent can criminal trials be expected to establish the truth about historic events for journalists? The question is a serious one, but it has been confounded by a discrepancy that exists between the legal and journalistic expectation of what a trial does. In law, the purpose of a criminal trial is to decide, according to predetermined rules, whether a defendant is guilty or not guilty of a particular charge. Adversary proceedings are designed to render a simple yes-or-no answer to some precise question, a question which has been drawn in as specific a manner as possible. In the popular imagination, however, a trial performs a somewhat grander service. It is looked upon as a fact-finding operation, an occasion for the public exposure of all known information regarding a given crime. The general assumption is that, if fairly conducted, a trial will yield the whole truth; aside from meting out justice to the accused, it will provide complete information and resolve the doubts of a concerned public.

The assumption that the "truth" ineluctably emerges in a fair trial is the premise of countless mystery novels and courtroom television dramas of the Perry Mason variety. It is a presupposition which is reinforced by the news media, a convenient tack for journalists to take, since it reduces the burden of reporting the facts about a crime to the business of covering court proceedings. "Objective journalism" requires only that both sides of a story be printed—a requirement that it is fulfilled by the contrapuntal presentation of evidence by prosecution and defense; in addition, cross-examination provides an element of dramatic conflict, neatly resolved by the jury's verdict.

A recent lead editorial in *The New York Times,* entitled "Tongue-Tied Justice," and written in reaction to James Earl Ray's decision to plead guilty to the murder of Dr. Martin Luther King, is a telling case in point. For Ray's decision had the effect of depriving the press of a long-anticipated trial, one which was expected to provide answers to the same sorts of questions which continue to disturb the public regarding the assassination of President Kennedy, and which presumably linger on because Lee Harvey Oswald was never brought to trial. The editorial is worth quoting at length:

The aborted trial of James Earl Ray for the assassination of Dr. Martin Luther King, Jr. is a shocking breach of faith with the American people, black and white, and of people the world over still numbed and puzzled by the gunfire that struck down this international leader.

Ray is entitled by all legal means to avail himself of the defenses open to him under the law. But by no means, legal or pragmatic, should the doors of the courtroom and the jail be slammed shut on the facts, the motives, and the doubts of this horrible murder.

Why should this assassination case be tried by statements instead of formal legal procedures, subject to examination and cross-examination, the presentation of all the evidence by the prosecution, the appearance of the accused in open court? . . . In the ghetto and in the world outside the ghetto, the question still cries for answer: Was there a conspiracy to kill Dr. King and who was in it?

The state's case has been read to the jury. But that is hardly enough in a case of this magnitude. This was not a street crime but, on the surface, a racist or quasi-political assassination. It is not enough to say that the state accepted the guilty plea and agreed to end the case because the death penalty has not been used since 1961 in Tennessee.

No one was demanding blood; everyone is demanding facts. Are we going to get the facts from Ray's lawyers, past or present, one of whom is trying to peddle the story to magazines? Are we going to get the facts from William Bradford Huie, the author who has "bought" the "rights" to Ray's story? What a mockery of justice for the facts to emerge in marketed justice!

Unless proceedings are convened in court—Federal, if not state—we shall never know the adjudicated truth. There should be no Warren Commissions necessary—a month or a year from now—to still our doubts and do what a Tennessee court has failed to do.

It is clear from this editorial that the *Times* does not consider it the function of a trial merely to determine whether the accused is guilty or not guilty; Ray's plea would have been sufficient for that purpose. The "mockery of justice" perpetrated by the Tennessee court lay not in its failure to provide due process for Ray but in its failure to provide information to the public: "facts," not "blood."

The rights of a defendant notwithstanding, the news media insist that a major trial be turned into a public forum. To accomplish that end, the accused must appear in open court, the prosecution must present all the evidence, cross-examination must take place, and "by no means, legal or pragmatic," should the courtroom doors be slammed shut on the facts. Naturally, a plea of guilty on the part of a defendant is therefore precluded, for it cuts short the issuance of facts and information. What the media do not appear to understand, however, is that a guilty plea is a defendant's *legal* prerogative. Nor do the media fully recognize the right of the accused *not* to take the stand but simply to remain mute, or the right of the defense to attack or attempt to contravert the prosecution's case *without* presenting its own side of the story, or the procedural rules which impose restrictions upon the sorts of evidence that may be introduced and which require that the prosecution present only such evidence as is relevant to the specific charges at hand. There can be no provision in law, furthermore, for differentiating between "routine" murder trials and extraordinary ones, such as "quasi-political assassination"; all must be governed by the same fixed rules, some of which necessarily impede the dis-

closure of information. Often the right of a defendant is precisely his right to withhold, or prevent
the prosecution from introducing, certain information which the public might like to know but
which might prove to be prejudicial to his case.

Where James Earl Ray is concerned, it is not
at all certain that a full-dress trial would have
provided any truly satisfying historical answers to
the mysteries of the King assassination. The
prosecution's case, which the jury had read before
the guilty plea was accepted, introduced no evidence that Ray had been party to a conspiracy.
The defense apparently had no intention of attempting to show that Ray had murdered Dr.
King at the behest of others; indeed, it would not
have made much sense for the defense to have
done so, since the fact of Ray's participation in a
conspiracy would in no way have affected the
murder charge. An open trial could only have
facilitated a judgment as to whether or not Ray
was guilty, as charged, of having fired the shot
that killed Dr. King.

In one of the few systematic efforts that have
been made to evaluate the fact-finding efficacy of
criminal trials, Professor Herbert Packer of Stanford Law School examined some of the more
prominent cases involving accused Communist
subversives during the McCarthy era;* he found
that a trial, considered as a means of establishing
historical truths, inevitably encounters one of two
problems: "either it leaves out too much to be

* *Ex-Communist Witnesses* (Palo Alto, Calif.: Stanford University Press, 1962).

informative or it includes too much to be orderly."
To be effective, a criminal charge must be drawn
as narrowly as possible. Rules of relevancy are
such that a complete historical exposition can
rarely emerge in the course of a trial. Even in cases
—like the Smith Act conspiracy trials—where a
great deal of information was allowed to be introduced, Packer found that the adversary process
"simply is not well adapted to the intelligible se-
quential ordering of complex factual information"; those bits and pieces that have emerged in
such trials fail to yield a comprehensive truth.
Packer concluded that the criminal trial, as an
instrument of fact-finding, was unequal to the demands placed upon it. Since most criminal trials
are settled by a guilty plea or by a plea negotiated
by the counsels, a comprehensive search for facts
is not called for, or needed. In "routine" cases,
ones that do not generate public controversy, the
verdict of the court is generally accepted, and soon
forgotten, by the public: the fact that a decision
has been rendered is more important than the nature of the verdict itself. It is only in the most
celebrated cases, usually those which touch upon
widely held political or moral convictions, and in
which the crime is linked to a larger symbolic
cause, that the verdict is likely to be challenged.
Yet even in such cases, the attack usually centers
upon the question of whether the court as an institution possesses the necessary fact-finding apparatus to determine satisfactory truths about a
complex event.

    In the United States, perhaps the trial most
thoroughly scrutinized for its "fairness' has been

that of Sacco and Vanzetti; for many people, this trial has become a kind of American version of the Dreyfus case. The common argument runs as follows: two Italian anarchists were arrested and convicted of murder, not because there was any substantial evidence against them, but because of a prevailing hysteria about, and prejudice against, anarchists, a prejudice shared by the court that tried them. Even though the trial was manifestly unfair, and the evidence transparently flimsy, the argument continues, the Establishment rallied to the defense of the verdict in an effort to protect the political system.

In 1927, the year that Sacco and Vanzetti were executed, the trial proceedings against the two men were vigorously attacked by Felix Frankfurter, then a professor of law at Harvard; scores of books and articles have since reiterated and expanded upon Frankfurter's basic theme that the trial was unfair.* Herbert B. Ehrmann, the last surviving defense lawyer who played a central role in the case, has written the latest, and what is no doubt the most comprehensive, analysis, not only of the trial, but of the crime as well.†

Ehrmann too argues that the conviction of two innocent men proceeded from an unfair trial and from the egregious errors of a prejudiced

---

*An excellent bibliography is available in G. Louis Joughlin and Edmund M. Morgan, *The Legacy of Sacco and Vanzetti* (Magnolia, Mass.: Peter Smith, 1964). A complete transcript of the trial and the subsequent proceedings, with a prefatory essay by William O. Douglas, has recently been issued in a six-volume reprint by Paul P. Appel, Inc.

†*The Case That Will Not Die: Commonwealth vs. Sacco and Vanzetti* (Boston: Little, Brown, 1969).

judge, but his trenchant analysis of the evidence, both that introduced into and that omitted from the trial, raises larger questions about the adequacy of the judicial process. For most of the evidence that Ehrmann, like others before him, has relied on to show that Sacco and Vanzetti were innocent of the crime was in fact never introduced during the trial. Some of this evidence, such as a convicted murderer's belated confession that his gang, and not Sacco and Vanzetti, were responsible for the crime, came to light only after the trial had ended. Other evidence, like the reports of the Pinkerton Detective Agency and the local police department, which cast considerable light on the way in which the case against Sacco and Vanzetti was constructed, were not entered into evidence by the prosecution because they were not relevant to the charges against the defendants. Agreements between defense and prosecution counsel led to the exclusion of still other evidence that might have further illuminated the case. Since a trial is not an investigative but a demonstrative proceeding, it can only evaluate the facts brought forth by the prosecution and defense. And, given the nature of the adversary system, in which each side attempts to develop evidence that is helpful to its side of the case and exclude evidence that is detrimental to it, there is little reason to expect that a trial, even a fair one, will produce all the evidence that exists.

Ehrmann demonstrates how the prosecutor's skillful cross-examination was used to confuse witnesses about events that took place more than a year before the trial, and to discredit the testimony of hostile witnesses. (Herbert Packer also found that cross-examination does not necessarily serve as a "great engine of truth" for eliciting the broad context of an event.) Ehrmann further indicates that "expert testimony" was not always the impartial scientific interpretation of evidence that it is presumed to be. The experts in the Sacco-Vanzetti trial made prior arrangements as to what they would be asked and how they would answer. In the testimony about ballistics, for example, a noted expert went to considerable lengths to find terms that would deliberately convey a *mis*-impression of his actual reading of the evidence. Some of the more telling ballistics evidence was also excluded by stipulations, or deals, between prosecution and defense. This is not to suggest that evidence that was excluded would always have worked to the defendants' benefit. A re-analysis of the ballistics evidence, for example, done six years after the trial with the newly developed comparison microscope, indicated that one of the murder bullets did indeed match the revolver found on Sacco at the time of his arrest.*

But in any event, the fact that data which may be vital to the determination of historical truth can be excluded from a trial does not necessarily mean that the trial is "unfair"—at least, not in the sense that the rules and procedures of law have been unfairly or improperly

---

*A more complete analysis of the ballistics evidence can be found in Francis Russell, *Tragedy in Dedham* (New York: McGraw-Hill, 1962).

applied. Quite the opposite may be the case: rules and procedures designed to protect the rights of the accused and facilitate the adversary process can, and often do, work to restrict the evidence that can be introduced. Nor can a trial, no matter how "fair," evaluate evidence that has been missed by the police investigations, which themselves may have been faulty or tendentious. The ability of the defense to conduct its own private investigation is limited by the resources available to it, both financial and legal, and by its purpose—to find data which support its client's side of the case. Even if the Sacco-Vanzetti trial had been a paragon of fair procedure, a true picture of the event might not have emerged in the course of it. To be sure, a fairer trial (which would have excluded *more,* not less, evidence) might have produced a verdict of not guilty, but that judgment would still have been made on the basis of incomplete information—for example, some of the incriminating ballistics evidence might have been disallowed for technical reasons—and there still could have been no certainty about the accuracy with which the trial had reconstructed the historic event.

A trial, then, can produce a decision of guilty or not guilty, and if the trial is assumed to have been fairly conducted, the decision will be generally accepted, but a trial cannot be counted on to yield large historic truths. Whether the doubts surrounding the King assassination will be resolved more reliably than those of the Sacco-Vanzetti case remains to be seen. But the nature of our judicial system is such that, when the investigative wherewithal of public agencies has been exhausted, the responsibility for providing the public with a full rendering of the event ultimately rests not with the courts, but with concerned historians.

—"Truth in the Courtroom"
Commentary, 1969

BROADCAST JOURNALISM: THE RATING GAME

The form that the news takes is shaped not only by the events and journalists but, perhaps more pervasively, by the requisites of the news organizations which predetermine the way journalistic talents are to be deployed, utilized, and limited. In the case of national television, the essential need of each network is to amass a huge national audience, as measured by the biweekly Nielsen ratings, which exceeds or is at least competitive with that of its rivals. The struggle of the ABC network to attain a competitive rating for its evening news service demonstrates the power of the nexus between ratings and news.

The Problem

In November 1969, ABC was running a poor third in its audience ratings. Whereas the rival CBS and NBC dinnertime news programs were each reaching some ten million homes, ABC's news was barely reaching four million homes, according to the Nielsen ratings. Such poor performance was not merely a matter of prestige loss for ABC: advertisers, whose rates vary according to the estimated audience for a program, were paying upwards of $25,000 a minute for commericals on NBC's and CBS's news, but only $8,000 a minute for equivalent time on ABC news (when it could be sold at all). The production costs for a half-hour of news was roughly the same for all three networks; the difference in revenue was, however, quite dramatic: $17,000 a minute (between that of CBS and ABC) multiplied by six minutes a night, five nights a week, added up to almost $20 million a year (even when advertising agency commissions were deducted). In the case of ABC in 1969, such a sum could make the difference between the entire network being profitable or unprofitable. With stakes as high as these, the crucial question was: How could network news substantially increase its audience?

Whereas a newspaper can raise its newsstand sales, and "circulation," by investing resources in its editorial products—i.e., scoops, exposés, exclusive interviews, features, and so forth—network news cannot as easily increase its audience directly by improving the content of its programs. This is because television networks, which were once aptly described by a network president as "nothing more than programs and telephone wires," are almost entirely dependent on affiliated stations in local markets to provide audiences for their programs. Aside from the five television stations which they are allowed to own and operate, each network contracts with some two hundred independently owned stations, or "affiliates," to rebroadcast its programs in their local markets in return for a share of the national advertising sold on the network programs. The affiliates are absolutely free, however, to refuse to broadcast, or "clear," any network program which they find unprofitable or "deem unsuitable" for any reason to carry in their schedule. (Technically, affiliates are permitted to carry the news programs of the other networks, but few carry more than one network's news. And as network news is usually less profitable than alternative local programming, this can be a serious problem. In 1969 forty-three ABC affiliates in the one hundred largest markets, including Boston, Cleveland, Cincinnati, Miami, and Houston, refused to clear the ABC Evening News (while its rivals had virtually 100 percent clearance). If affiliates don't carry a program, it is impossible for it to achieve a high national audience rating, regardless of the effectiveness of its presentation of the news. As NBC president Richard C. Wald observed, "Huntley, Brinkley and Cronkite could sing, dance or strip in their New York studios, but if affiliates didn't choose to take the show, it wouldn't raise an eyebrow." Affiliates, moreover, affect the size of the audience by their decision on when to schedule the news. ABC "feeds" its half-hour news program at 6, 6:30 and 7 P.M. EST, and each affiliate can thus choose when to show the program in its local market.* In 1969 a large number of ABC affiliates preferred to show the program at 6 P.M.—a time when there usually were fewer viewers watching television. The problem was compounded by the fact that this was a time when ABC's news competed with entertainment programs rather than the other network newscasts. Since entertainment almost invariably outdraws a news program—especially in the early evening when there are a large number of children in the audience—this early scheduling strongly diminished the possibility of the ABC News receiving ratings comparable to those of the other networks' news programs. (Even in news-conscious New York City, all three network news programs, though they are shown at 7 P.M., trail entertainment programs on the independent channels.)

Not only are the networks dependent on affiliates for clearing and favorably scheduling their newscasts, but affiliates are expected to provide the vital "lead-in" audience for it. Network executives generally agree that network newscasts themselves attract only a fraction of their audience, and "inherit" most of it from viewers who tune in for local news or entertainment shows. As one ABC audience expert explained, "Most viewers care most about local sports and weather, and what's happening in their locality. National news

*NBC and CBS have only two feeds at 6:30 and 7:00 P.M.

holds much less immediate interest for them." This accounts for the fact that the same network news programs vary sharply from city to city in their popularity. As CBS News president Richard Salant explained, "You'll find a general correlation between the audience of network news broadcasts and local news broadcasts—and probably the local news is the decisive thing." This was particularly true of ABC News in 1969, when an "in depth" audience study showed that only a small percentage of those who watched the Evening News were attracted by the program itself.

To be sure, the quality of a network news program helps to maintain the already existing audience. It is generally assumed by network executives that if a newscast is technically flawed, confusing, too slowly paced, or visually offensive, viewers will turn to another channel. And as their six-figure annual salaries indicate, it is assumed that "star" anchormen, by dint of the constancy of their personality, help retain the loyalty of a large share of the audience. (Even a superstar like Walter Cronkite, who ranks head and shoulders above all others in audience-preference ratings, cannot "carry" his audience with him. When ABC and CBS switched affiliates in Boston in March 1972, the audience for CBS News with Cronkite declined almost 40 percent.

The Strategy

Before a network need worry about retaining a news audience, it must first marshal one, and in ABC's case, this required persuading affiliates in key markets to clear or reschedule the Evening News. In 1969 ABC thus embarked on a new campaign to win the cooperation of its affiliates. There are, of course, a number of arguments why it is in the self-enlightened interest of an affiliate to use, or "clear," network news: the Federal Communications Commission (FCC) looks more favorably on stations' license renewal applications if they clear network news; network news improves the "news image" of a station in a community and thereby enhances the local news programs; and by clearing network news, affiliates greatly add to the economic health of the parent network, which, in turn, permits it to acquire better sports and entertainment programming. However, all these reasons were equally valid before 1969—and, if anything, more cogent, as ABC was then losing more money—yet these reasons had always failed to persuade key affiliates to clear the Evening News. To gain the cooperation of these affiliates, it was thus decided that ABC had to radically transform its news program and create a highly competitive "alternative" to the other two nightly networks newscasts. One main objective, as ABC News vice-president William Sheehan noted in an earlier memorandum, would be "to make ABC Evening News different enough in its presentation to attract attention away from its competitors." And while "differentiating" its newscast from that of the other networks, an ABC executive explained, another objective was to make it more acceptable to affiliates.

The actual tactics for achieving these strategic ends were less clearly articulated. But after

Vice-President Agnew openly attacked the "fairness" of network news, one selling point—at least to some recalcitrant affiliates—evolved that ABC would be "fairer" in its treatment of the news than the rival networks. In 1970 Elmer Lower, the president of ABC News, informed the affiliates that detailed "content analysis" done shortly after Agnew's speech by an independent consultant had indicated that in 1969 on ABC News "news tending to support the administration viewpoint totaled 12 hours, 39 minutes; news likely to displease Nixon supporters, 10 hours, 18 minutes; neutral news, 8 hours, 18 minutes." Affiliates were also told that "this content analysis survey is continuing." ABC further separated itself from the other networks on the issues that Agnew raised when Howard K. Smith, ABC's star commentator, wrote in *TV Guide* in early 1970: "I agree with some of what Mr. Agnew said. . . . The networks have ignored this situation, despite years of protest, because they have power." (S.P. Hesmen for the other networks vigorously attacked Agnew's speech.) And less openly, high ABC executives made it clear to affiliates that their newscast was looked on more favorably by the White House than its competitors. The "opening to the right," as a disgruntled ABC correspondent described the shift, was defined to affiliates as an effort to "balance" administration views against criticisms, while the other networks were less fair in this respect.

The message was not lost on the owners of affiliates. "Their politics are Republican, their ideals are pragmatic and their preoccupation with return on invested capital and the safety of their license to broadcast is total," a NBC executive wrote in a memo on affiliate relations in 1969. While this picture of affiliates may be too darkly drawn, many ABC affiliates were in fact becoming increasingly concerned in 1969 with the tenure of their licenses, especially after the Agnew attack, and the promise that special pains would be taken to "balance" the news on ABC was generally well received. Almost all the sixteen affiliate executives I spoke with cited the "balance" in ABC News as one of the chief reasons why, after 1969, they decided to clear it. There were, of course, other inducements: in some cases, ABC tied the availability of highly desired programs, such as *Marcus Welby* or National League football, with clearance of the news; in other cases, higher "compensation" was offered to the stations; and the FCC helped by sending out a questionnaire in 1969 to all licensees that asked, in effect, for an explanation of why affiliates were not carrying network news. But according to affiliate executives, in most cases it was the revision in the content of the program itself which persuaded reluctant affiliates to carry it. For example, Lawrence "Bud" Rogers, the president of Taft Broadcasting Corporation, which owns and operates important ABC affiliates in Cincinnati, Columbus, Birmingham, and Scranton, explained, "One reason we finally cleared ABC News was they gave us a real alternative to the other network news programs." The other networks were, in his opinion, "tilted left" and "poorly balanced" in their news coverage and "arrogant" in responding to White House and congressional criticism; ABC, on the other hand, "does a superior job in terms of fairness and balance and is judicious in considering political criticism." Before ABC completely revamped its newscast in 1969, Rogers said he preferred to "counterprogram" the other network news programs with *The Merv Griffin Show,* an entertainment program. Don Perris, the vice-president of the ABC affiliate in Cleveland, gave a similiar explanation: "Before '69, there was little to recommend their [news] show. Then they turned the whole news department around and put on the fairest and best news show on the air. . . . Balance was a terrifically important factor in our taking the program. . . . Our regular audience surveys now give it the highest marks for fairness, and we never have any complaints." And a Southern affiliate executive, who preferred to remain anonymous, said, "The fact that they were obviously considered the best network by the White House entered into our decision [to clear the Evening News]." The ABC affiliate relations department makes no secret about the fact that "the tone and balance of the news" helped win affiliate cooperation. Indeed, by 1970 ABC was able to report to its affiliates that the news had been "restructured to meet the changing needs and desires of the viewing public."

The Revision

To bring about this "restructuring" of the news, ABC News president Elmer Lower initiated three decisive changes: Avram Westin, a former CBS producer, who had recently come to ABC, was given carte blanche powers to totally revise the "news concept"; a large amount of money was invested in "attitudinal surveys" of the news audience, which were conducted by the firm of McHugh and Hoffman on a continuous basis; and in 1970, Harry Reasoner was hired away from CBS for a salary of $250,000 a year to create the anchorman team of "Smith and Reasoner." Lower pointed out that these steps were taken "as part of an overall strategy to create a really competitive news service."

Av Westin had acquired a reputation among colleagues for having an unsurpassed talent for "combining news and showmanship," as one of them put it. When he produced the CBS Morning News in 1963, and faced the inherent difficulty of creating the appearance of fast-breaking news at a time in the morning when usually there existed only the previous day's news film, Westin "showed a real genius for making old stories appear new and interesting," according to one former colleague.

When Westin reviewed the audience studies prepared by McHugh–Hoffman, he found that the Evening News had to be directed essentially at "a lower class and older audience" which was as much interested in being entertained as receiving reports on the day's events. In probing the "in depth" reactions in a cross-section of viewers, while they watched taped replays of the newscast, ABC's audience experts concluded that the "critical factor in heightening the entertainment value of a news show" was filmed stories, and preferably ones that depicted the "benevolent activities of youths, blacks and other segments of societies." While these types of "constructive" human-interest stories were found to satisfy the mass audience, stories which stressed the "problematic" nature of news, and unresolved controversy, tended to confuse, bore, and lose viewers.

"A television news broadcast can be produced in any number of different ways," Westin noted. "Every executive producer should have a concept before he begins and it is up to him to translate that concept into the reality of approximately thirty minutes of moving pictures, slides, maps, graphics, anchormen, field correspondents' reports and, hopefully, commercials." (Actually, if the six minutes of commercials and the time necessary for affiliate and network identification are deducted from this total, there are only about twenty-two minutes of air time left for news in a "thirty-minute program.") The "concept" with which Westin began required completely redesigning the format of the program. Together with Ben Blank, the highly imaginative ABC art director, Westin fashioned a set of highly graphic symbols and comic-book-style bubbles, with "key quotes" inside them, to serve as a backdrop for the anchormen as they reported news developments. For example, a clenched black fist symbolized Black Protest (while a red fist stands for Youth Protest); a plane in the shape of an American flag symbolizes American bombing; three strands of barbed wire symbolized prisoners of war; a schoolhouse, half-black, half-white, symbolizes civil rights issues, and the outline of a television set stands appropriately for media issues. The symbol, which appears on the screen behind the commentator, provides a sort of leitmotif to help viewers instantly recognize the "overall theme of the narrative being constructed," Westin explains. This is designed to overcome what Westin calls the "understandability factor," or "the problem of dealing with a mass audience." These visual simplifications also served to tie together diverse pieces of information under a single symbolic heading, or "umbrella." For instance, a number of separate incidents involving attacks on police could be "integrated" under the graphic symbol of a bull's-eye target, with bullet holes in it, superimposed over a silhouette of a policeman.

And because the Evening News audience is presumed to have a very limited span of attention, Westin also decided to limit the length of a report to under three minutes, even if it meant dividing a segment into three separate stories on three aspects of it. Westin wrote: "Stories—both film and anchorman's scripted on-camera material—are combined into a logical thread, leading the audience through the news so that their distracted minds do not have to make sharp twists and turns to follow what is going on."

Changing the format, style, and pace of the program was only part of the job. To achieve the sort of political balance the affiliates—and network executives—were promised, Westin had to basically revise the processes of collecting and presenting the news. This, in turn, required tight control over the news operation. For one thing, Westin insisted that all scripts be Telexed to New

York. "Ad-libbing" was deemed strictly "unacceptable." All the anchormen's introductions to stories were to be written by producers in New York or Washington directly under Westin's supervision; and field reports were to be written so that they didn't "fight" these "lead-ins." The graphic background symbol and key quote were to be personally selected by Westin, which provided another element of visual control. In short, almost all aspects of the news report—from the initial assignment to the final editing—were to be superintended by Westin.

To effectively "alter the focus" of ABC News' coverage of such issues as Vietnam, Westin needed to control not only the editing process but also the advance assignment of stories. In his first letter to correspondents on March 14, 1969, Westin wrote, "I am operating on the theory that a producer should be aggressive and 'produce' a broadcast, not waiting for news to happen in order to scramble after it. Anticipating events is most important." In the next two weeks, he further listed the subjects on which he wanted stories and ordered the Saigon bureau to seek stories on the theme of "the eventual pull-out of the American forces." By ordering stories for the "bank," or the stockpile of timeless stories kept in reserve, he also exerted advance control over coverage. For example, in June of 1970 he suggested that stories about "black rioting, looting and marching" were becoming part and parcel of a "cliché"; thus, rather than preparing advance stories on this theme, he suggested centering stories on the theme of the collapse of services: "trains that do not run, mail that isn't delivered, garbage collections that are not made, inadequate hospitals, no doctors, reading scores that are lower, etc." And while he suggested that some correspondents might want to challenge the "A. Westin thesis," he effectively ordered advance reports on these subjects "so that when we are confronted with events this summer, we can go to the 'Bank' . . ." As one former NBC correspondent explained, "Things were tightly run at NBC . . . , but here almost every story is commissioned by Westin." (Westin claimed to have initiated between 50 and 60 percent of such discretionary stories.)

Since a main objective is to "differentiate" ABC News from the other network news programs, Westin not only selects the subjects that are to be covered, but he also attempts to preordain the direction, or "thrust," of stories on controversial subjects. In a remarkably frank interview on Steven Scheuer's program *All About Television* in 1973, Westin explained, "I believe that there is this nuance in the way that pieces can be constructed, and I believe that by varying the thrust of the way we do the reportage in these expository pieces you can achieve a different way, a different type of fairness, and a different type of balance." The "different way" referred to replacing the "Eastern liberal way" with the "Middle America" position as the starting point of news stories. He explained on the same program: "Instead of the accepted . . . 'Eastern Liberal' position answer, rather than give them first stab." Westin further explained this to me as "a conscious policy of reversing perspectives," and cited, as an example of this, his treatment of the abortion issue: "On the other networks, there is a clichéd formula for doing abortion stories," he explained. "This might be called the Eastern Liberal syndrome. You begin by showing film of unwanted children in a hospital, a voice-over narration gives essentially the liberal position: 'These unwanted children exist because we don't have liberalized abortion laws.' An advocate of abortion reform is then put on to reinforce this position. Finally, a balancing interview with an old fogey is put on, who says 'Abortion is wrong,' and a correspondent sums it up by saying, 'A controversy still exists.'" To "reverse perspectives," Westin continues, "I order the correspondent to start with pictures of destroyed fetuses, or their equivalent, with a voice-over narration saying that 'abortion has resulted in this death,' and then put on an interview with an advocate of the present abortion laws calling for 'the respect of life.' Then we put on the balancing interview with a critic of the abortion laws, and make her answer these charges." This policy of "reversing perspectives," even though it may involve no more than allowing a pro-administration spokesman to state his case first and a critic to have the reply, makes a real, if subtle, difference in the presentation of the news, since the other networks usually allow the critic to "have the first bite." For example, whereas NBC and CBS newscasts on the dismantling of the Office of Economic Opportunity (OEO) began with reports about poverty workers who would lose their jobs because of the planned cuts of the Nixon administration, the ABC News on February 16, 1973, began with an interview with Howard Phillips, the OEO director, who defended the plans to eliminate the office.

While a number of ABC correspondents find that these "reverse perspectives" amount to little more than "slanting the news to the right," affiliate managers and network executives praised Westin for "eliminating the leftward slant," as one phrased it. Westin himself considered affiliate relations an important part of his job. When one affiliate owner complained last March that a correspondent had made a "left jab" on President Nixon's Vietnam policy, Westin replied with a detailed analysis of the script and concluded: "There was no 'left jab' intended or delivered. . . . I hope my rather lengthy explanation will satisfy your justifiable concern that television news remain unbiased."

Moreover, if any story seems to favor one side of a controversy over the other, it became Westin's declared policy to seek out and present a "balancing piece" within seven broadcast days. As he wrote a concerned affiliate, "We . . . do our best to play it right down the middle." Except for the portions of the program clearly labeled "Commentary," correspondents are prohibited from stating a conclusion in their reporting. In one exceptional incident, one new ABC correspondent, Lem Tucker, insisted on assigning blame in the crash of an airplane into Chicago housing on a government agency, and to his surprise, found the label "Commentary" superimposed over his image from New York. More usually, the "commentaries" are given at the end of the program by the anchormen, after they have been approved by vice-president William Sheehan.

The final element in the strategy fell into

place in late 1970, when ABC acquired the services of Harry Reasoner, a long-time CBS newscaster whose personal popularity rating among the audience was second only to Walter Cronkite. Up to that point, the ABC Evening News had been anchored by Frank Reynolds in New York and Howard K. Smith in Washington. Smith had shown up in the audience studies as the only ABC newsman with "star" qualities; Reynolds had relatively little popularity among ABC viewers—according to the studies, he was perceived of as being "cold" and "impersonal." So ABC had been looking for a more authoritative and appealing commentator, and when Reasoner decided not to renew his CBS contract, Lower explained, "We jumped at the opportunity. Reasoner replaced Reynolds, and the "Smith-Reasoner" anchor team was created. Together, Smith and Reasoner proved an immediate success, with affiliates as well as the audience. With very few exceptions, all of the ABC affiliates now clear the Evening News, and many have moved it to a more favorable position in their schedule. The total audience rose from less than 4 million homes in 1969 to 7.4 million homes in the first quarter of 1973. The price per minute for commercials also rose dramatically from an average of $8,000 a minute to $18,000 in 1973. In fact, by almost every measure employed by networks, ABC News could be judged a stunning success. (And Westin was promoted to vice-president in 1973.) ABC had succeeded in the rating game but only at a cost of completely changing its journalistic product.

THE PROBLEM
OF BIAS IN
TELEVISION NEWS

The issue of bias in television news often tends to be reduced to the closely related issue of personal bias: Are individual newsmen fair or unfair in their treatment of the news? For example, in a congressional conference on the media in 1973, Theodore Koop, a vice-president of CBS News, defined and disposed of the issue of a bias by saying, "I suggest the bias lies in the eye of the beholder rather than the newsman. . . . Walter Cronkite, and his opposite numbers, didn't get where they are by being biased." Since no one at the conference had any interest in impeaching the integrity of Cronkite, the issue was effectively foreclosed. The twin issues of news bias and personal bias are not inseparable, however. News can be biased even if newsmen are personally fair and unbiased. Just as a roulette wheel mounted on a tilted table tends to favor some numbers over other numbers, no matter how fair the croupier might be, a television network "tilted" in a consistent direction because of the way it is organized will also tend to favor certain types of stories over others, no matter how fair the newscaster might be. To be sure, personal bias exists on network news—even if its extent is greatly exaggerated—but it may be more the symptomatic effect, rather than the cause, of the network leaning in certain directions. Newsmen, after all, have only limited control over their product: producers determine the stories they are assigned to cover, the length and form of their reports, and the editing of their final product. Av Westin, now vice-president of ABC News, described the process of control quite candidly in a memorandum:

The senior producers decide if the story has been adequately covered and they also estimate how long the report should be run. In most cases, correspondents deliberately overwrite their scripts giving the producer at home the option of editing it down: selecting which portions of interviews are to be used and which elements in the narration are to be kept and which are to be discarded. . . . In some cases, the senior producer "salvages" a report by assigning the correspondent to redo his narration or by sending a cameraman to refilm a sequence.

In such a situation, correspondents have little opportunity to insert personal values in news stories that run counter to the network's interest or objectives—(especially if they want to receive further assignments. Anchormen and commentators are even more tightly controlled as to what they say on or off camera. And while they are attacked by the President of the United States because of their putative power to distort issues, they are not uncommonly deprecated in the newsroom as "player pianos" because almost all of their material is written for them by producers and writers, and (in the case of commentators) approved by executives.

In practice, it is usually not necessary to control newsmen through tight editorial and writing supervision: the networks' policies of recruitment and advancement assure that only newsmen that give precedence to organizational over personal values will succeed in network news. Theodore Koop was therefore quite correct in pointing out that Cronkite did not rise to prominence at CBS by espousing personal biases. Indeed, all three networks act to filter out correspondents who have a high degree of personal commitment on issues, or appear to the audience to have a "bias," and advance correspondents who hold or adopt a style of presenting the news that fits the networks' requisites.

The public's constant search for "personal bias" in newsmen, even if not totally chimerical, tends to obscure a far more pervasive form of "organizational bias" flowing from the subsurface contours and tilts that underlie network news and lead newsmen in certain consistent directions. Rather than asking, "How are newsmen biased?" —a question that inevitably leads to a bottomless morass of disputed examples and counter-examples—it would seem far more profitable to ask, "In what ways do the networks tend to bias the news?" Presumably, television networks, like any other business organization, must fulfill certain basic requirements to survive in a competitive world, and their news operation must be organized so that it does not undercut these needs. And while they are in somewhat different situations, all three network news operations have very similar requisites: they must maintain, if not add to, a national audience; their programs must be acceptable to affiliated (but independently owned) stations in all the major cities in the United States; the presentation of news must conform to the ground rules laid down by the Federal Communications Commission (FCC), which regulates broadcasting; and the entire process of gathering, editing, and disseminating the news must be done within a fixed budget. At any network, if a producer or news executive allows any of these organization values to be consistently violated (if the audience declines, if affiliates complain or refuse to "clear" the news in a favorable time period, if the FCC takes unfavorable action, or if production costs exceed the budget), he will most likely be replaced. "Network news is a game with strict rules," Av Westin explained. "A producer can't change the rules, he simply tries to recognize them and play better by them than his competitors." But while executives, producers and newsmen may have little choice in the matter, following the "rules" ineluctably tilts the news toward certain types of stories and modes of presentation, and away from others.

Audience

While the prime requisite is to maintain a mass audience, audience studies at all three networks consistently show that the vast preponderance of viewers whose attention must be retained for a half-hour of national news are watching television at that hour for the entertainment programs that either precede or follow the news, not for the news itself. Moreover, of those who tune in for news, most are interested in the local report—weather, sports, or a fire on Main Street—not in the national happenings reported by the network. As the president of CBS News pointed out, network news is simply "salted in" at a time when most viewers are watching television for other reasons. Network news therefore cannot simply report the events of the day in the order of their presumed importance, as *The New York Times* can do; it must transmute selected events into "stories" that would interest a mass audience that is not presumably interested in the news itself. Irving Kristol perceptively captured the problem facing network producers when he wrote: "Tabloid journalism . . . neatly sums up the essence of television news. Its bent is toward an intense focusing upon melodramatic situations." To be effective, then, as Reuven Frank, the former president of NBC News, suggested, network news must transform a news item about declining farm prices into a story about a family watching with choked tears as their farm is auctioned off to pay their debts.

Nor can the stories be overly complex. Audience studies also show that viewers of network news have fewer years of formal education than the population as a whole, and therefore can be expected to have less contextual or background knowledge than a more highly educated audience. This, in any case, is the theory to which most producers subscribe. Network news stories must therefore be self-contained: there must be a beginning in which the protagonists are identified in a few words and pictures, a climax in which some visual action takes place, and a denouement in which the conflict is resolved.

Finally, to retain the interest of a national audience stretching from Maine to Hawaii, network news must be constructed around visual elements that have universal appeal. For example, fires, riots, bloodshed, and armed confrontations, no matter where they occur, can be comprehended at a very basic level by viewers in all parts of the country. Producers and assignment editors, when they have a choice, thus seek out stories that can be illustrated by such visual action. An NBC producer explained that there is a "threefold distillation of action" in network news: producers seek action-filled stories, cameramen seek the moments of action that occur within a story, and then film editors intensify the action by cutting out "dead," or inactive, scenes.

The willy-nilly result of fulfilling the requisite for audience interest is that network news stories tend to be highly simplified melodramas, built around conflict, and illustrated with visual action. Since these truncated versions of reality omit details, qualifications, and contingencies, they make change appear to be deceptively simple (one side simply has to overwhelm another side in a confrontation). Although this bias toward change is not ideologically motivated but an inevitable outcome of the search for a mass audience, it tends to situate newsmen, who must describe the film story, in what appears to be a "liberal" position of endorsing reform.

Affiliates

A second requisite of network news is to maintain a "lineup" of affiliates. Networks each own only five stations—the limit allowed by law. They are heavily dependent on affiliated stations to carry their programming in most cities. Affiliates, however, cannot be compelled to carry any network programs which they deem not to be in the "public interest" (or, in effect, their private interest). Persuading affiliates to carry network news at a favorable time is an especially difficult task, since news is usually not as profitable as other programming they could otherwise carry. (In the case of ABC, the problem affected the profitability of the entire network.) If not for profit, affiliates subscribe to network news to obtain a "national news" program to complement their local newscasts (and thereby enhance their public service record in the eyes of the FCC). It is imperative, therefore, that the networks structure their news operation so that they produce a form of "national news" that is qualitatively different from the local news produced by the affiliates. As one NBC producer put it, "The basic job of network news is to nationalize news." At one level, this is accomplished simply by focusing coverage on the President, who in a very real sense is the only truly non-local actor on the national stage, and others involved in Presidential politics. But while Presidential politics fits in with the "national news" requisite, it accounts for only a small proportion of the daily news. Other events must be "nationalized," or somehow divorced from the local context and conditions in which they occur (obviously, all news occurs in some locality). The usual way in which network news producers routinely accomplish this difficult feat of converting local happenings to national stories is to organize a number of reports around a common theme. For example, two or more stories which depict violence in different cities can be fused into a single "national story" on the "urban crisis." Since the themes are chosen by a small group of producers in New York City, they tend to reflect the issues and trends that are of concern to a particular universe of persons in New York City. Producers who tend to read the same newspapers (particularly *The New York Times*) and news magazines, commute to the same area of the city, and discuss with friends the same agenda of problems can be expected to share a similar perspective on the critical themes of the day. The organizational requirement for "national news" thus not only leads to an unintended bias toward generalizing news (i.e., editing out the more specific local elements of stories while retaining universal elements), but also tends to result in diverse news events being organized around a limited number of themes predetermined by New York producers.

The Fairness Requisite

Unlike the print media, broadcasting is regulated by the federal government, which means, in short, that licensees of television and radio stations must conform to the ground rules laid down by the FCC or risk the tenure of their licenses. The FCC regulation which most affects the content and form of the news itself is the so-called fairness doctrine, which requires that if a controversial issue is discussed at all, an opposing view must also be presented in a reasonable time period. Network producers routinely come to grips with this ground rule by creating a "pro and con" model of reporting in which correspondents first present the "news" side of an issue (i.e., the happening which is the stimulus for the story), and then present a spokesman for the "other side" (which correspondents are responsible for seeking out). To avoid complaints, network policy also requires that the spokesmen for various causes be articulate and generally presentable. Network news thus tends to present most problems as a point-counter-point debate, between what appears to be equally matched opponents, which is not resolved. The result is that network news tends to show a divided society rather than the resolution of issues.

The Economic Requisite

Network news is an integral part of a much larger business: television networks. At all three networks, the news division is allocated a fixed amount of programming time and money for its operations. While these limits can be exceeded in extraordinary circumstances, producers are expected to conform to their budget in the long run. (At ABC, for example, each week the network's financial officer sends the news producers a graph depicting the discrepancy, if any, between budgeted expenses and actual expenses; producers then must explain the gap.)

Budgetary controls shape the news, though unintentionally, in some fairly consistent directions. For one thing, news stories cost significantly less if they are taken from some cities than from other cities. This is because the networks maintain permanent lines between some cities, such as New York and Washington, D.C., and no charge is made against the producers' budget for transmitting stories taken from such "free cities." On the other hand, special lines have to be rented from most other cities, such as Atlanta, Boston, or Los Angeles, to directly "feed" stories back to the networks' broadcasting centers in New York City. The charges for renting lines and connections for a single story can be as high as $4,000—or a considerable piece of the program's weekly budget. Producers can thus control their budgets, especially when other expenses are high, by omitting stories from cities which are more expensive to transmit from. "No one misses what he doesn't see," one NBC producer explained. A major story will rarely be sacrificed for budgetary reasons, but when producers have a choice between covering the same sort of an event, such as a student strike, in New York or in San Jose, California—and both seem equally capable of illustrating a national theme—there is a strong tendency to choose the New York story, which will do less damage to the weekly budget. In practice, this means that most of the immediate news on all three networks is taken from a handful of cities—principally New York, Washington, D.C., and Chicago—where the networks maintain permanent facilities. Since these particular cities are also highly cosmopolitan cities, which tend to be the center for groups demanding changes and reforms in the distribution of power in America, network news tends by structure rather than design to focus on the activities of these groups.

These few examples are not meant to fully explicate the effect of network organizations on the content of the news.* They do demonstrate, however, that much of what is presumed by former Vice-President Spiro Agnew and others to be an "Eastern-Liberal bias" on the part of newsmen is a more serious and less correctable matter than personal bias. For the most persistent distortions in network news flow not from the choice of newsmen or even producers, but from the survival requisites of the networks, which cannot easily be changed.

*A fuller attempt is made in my book *News from Nowhere* (New York: Random House, 1973).

THE
TELEVISED WAR

In 1973, after the United States agreed to withdraw from Vietnam, *TV Guide* asked me to review kinescopes and transcripts of the nightly coverage of the war by all three networks from 1962 to 1973.

From 1962 to 1973, almost nightly, Americans witnessed the war in Vietnam, on television. Never before in history has a nation allowed its citizens to view uncensored scenes of combat, destruction, and atrocities in their living rooms, in living color. Since television has become the principal—and most believed—source of news for most Americans, it is generally assumed that the constant exposure of this war on television was instrumental in shaping public opinion. It has become almost a truism, and the standard rhetoric of television executives, to say that television, by showing the terrible truth of war, caused the disillusionment of Americans with the war.

For example, at the height of the antiwar protest in 1967, NBC News producer Robert J. Northshield, in an interview with *The New York Times,* claimed, "TV is directly responsible for 125,000 people showing up at the UN Plaza to demonstrate against the war." James Hagerty, the former press secretary to President Dwight Eisenhower and currently a vice-president of ABC, has said, "By showing war in its stinking reality, we have taken away the glory and shown that negotiation is the only way to solve international problems."

This has also been the dominant view of those governing the nation during the war years, and it was perhaps most clearly articulated by Lyndon Baines Johnson. President Johnson stated in an article prepared for the *Encyclopaedia Britannica* in 1969 that unexpurgated coverage of the war on television "made the reality of the war more vivid" and thereby "may also have intensified the public's frustration over not being able to finish it off quickly."

Depending on whether the appraisal has come from hawk or dove, television has thus been either blamed or applauded for the disillusionment of the American public with the war.

The logical problem with this view is that an overwhelming majority of the American public *did* approve of the war in Vietnam (if public opinion polls are to be believed) during the first six years it was televised, from 1962 to 1967. The Gallup "trend" poll, for example, indicates that until mid-1967 the number of Americans who agreed with the decision to send American ground troops to Vietnam actually increased, despite television's coverage. To be sure, public opinion polls are, at best, only general indicators of the public's attitudes on narrowly defined questions; yet, in the case of Vietnam, almost every major poll taken through 1967 showed widespread support for American involvement in the war.

The issue of television's influence was more directly tested by a Harris poll in 1967, commissioned by *Newsweek* magazine. Through a series of questions, the poll attempted to determine the extent to which television intensified the public's opposition to the war. The surprising result was that 64 percent of the nationwide sample said that television's coverage made them *more* supportive of the American effort, and only 26 percent said that it had intensified their opposition to the war. Newsweek's conclusion was that "TV had encouraged a decisive majority of viewers to support the war."

This presents a paradox. Television frequently demonstrates that it has the power to shock and shape public opinion, as it did, for example, when it showed the nation the shootings at Kent State in 1970. Why did it not have a similar effect on public opinion after showing the nation the Vietnam war for a period longer than that of any other war in American history? This apparent contradiction rests on the assumption that television was more or less constant in exposing the horror and futility of the Vietnam war. In other words, one tends to assume that the Vietnam war was covered, and exposed, with the same vigilance and skepticism in the critical years of commitment

(1962–1967) as it has been in the last stages of protest and withdrawal (1969–1973).

In reviewing the 1962–72 nightly newscasts of the three networks, which provided the great bulk of Vietnam coverage, it becomes manifestly clear that this assumption is not warranted; television was neither monolithic nor consistent in its coverage and commentaries on the war. As the Indochina war wore on, the nature of the televised war dramatically changed—as did public opinion. To understand how television affected public opinion—and especially why a "decisive majority" claimed that television increased their support for the war—it is necessary to reexamine the various phases of the televised war.

Almost every discussion of television's early coverage of the war touches on what has been rightly called, by CBS News executive William Small, "the single most famous bit of reporting in South Vietnam"—the burning of the huts at Cam Ne. On August 5, 1965, the CBS Evening News carried a dramatic film story, narrated by Morley Safer, which showed U.S. Marines using their cigarette lighters to set fire to Vietnamese thatched huts in the village of Cam Ne. The report immediately became a cause célèbre. While the Assistant Secretary of Defense for Public Affairs, Arthur Sylvester, launched a semiofficial campaign to discredit the television story and vilify the correspondent as "unpatriotic," CBS executives, led by Fred W. Friendly, defended the story with equal vigor and proposed it for every available journalistic award.

The fact that this particular journalistic endeavor is now celebrated by virtually everyone who writes on the subject does not, however, mean that it exemplified the coverage of the war during this period. On the contrary, in examining network newscasts and scripts from 1962 to 1968, I could find few other comparable instances of indiscriminate American destruction or brutality (even though hundreds of South Vietnamese villages were destroyed and evacuated in "relocation programs" during this period). The same conclusion was reached also by Professor Lawrence Litchy of the University of Wisconsin, who systematically analyzed network kinescopes of this period. Professor Litchy concludes that instances, such as Cam Ne, shown on television of American brutality toward the South Vietnamese "could be counted on one hand." If the Cam Ne story is famous for being the exception to the rule, what, actually, was the public watching night after night on network newscasts?

Although American troops had been involved in the fighting in Vietnam since 1961, television coverage was extremely limited—sporadic, at best—until the networks assigned full-time film crews and correspondents to Vietnam in mid-1963. Prior to 1963 most of the reporting was done by the newscast anchormen, who generally treated the fighting in Vietnam as simply another outbreak in the cold war in which the United States was expected, in John F. Kennedy's words, "to help any friend, fight any foe." The Vietcong were commonly identified as "Reds" or "Communist terrorists" acting on orders from the Kremlin or "the Sino-Soviet bloc," rather than as partici-

pants in a civil war. Coverage of the first years of
the war was summed up by NBC correspondent
Floyd Kalber, who said in an NBC special on
Vietnam: "To the degree that we in the media paid
any attention at all to that small, dirty war in those
years, we almost wholly reported the position of
the Government."

And up until 1965, the network anchormen
seemed unanimous in support of American objectives in Vietnam. Some commentators, such as
NBC's Chet Huntley and ABC's Howard K.
Smith, remained "hawks," as they described
themselves, until the end. Even Walter Cronkite,
who later became a symbol of the disenchantment
with the war, earlier (in 1965) strongly endorsed
"the courageous decision that Communism's advance must be stopped in Asia and that guerrilla
warfare as a means to a political end must be
finally discouraged."

In late 1963, television did fully report the
repression of the Buddhists in Vietnam by the
Diem government. Like the other media, television in its stories from Saigon tended to be extremely critical of Diem and his family, who were
accused of impeding the struggle against the Communists. In August 1963, Huntley quoted U.S.
Army commanders as saying, "Diem washed
eighteen months of effort down the drain." And in
October 1963, Huntley summed up the anti-Diem
reporting on television when he said, "We journalists have found the Diem regime guilty of serving
Communism."

The opposition to Diem was thus not tan-
tamount to opposition to U.S. involvement in Vi-

etnam. Indeed, as the Pentagon Papers have fully established, it was U.S. policy in 1963 to discredit and dispose of the Diem regime so that the war could be more effectively prosecuted. When Diem was finally assassinated in November 1963, the change of governments was unanimously praised by network newsmen, who expressed the hope that "we can now get on with the war," as Huntley put it.

During the following year, the news on television was dominated heavily by the fact-finding missions of such authorities as Secretary of Defense Robert S. McNamara and General Maxwell Taylor, and by constant reports on the changing political situation in Saigon. After the attack by North Vietnamese torpedo boats on American destroyers in the Gulf of Tonkin in August 1964, virtually all the network commentators spoke approvingly of President Johnson's decision to retaliate by limited bombing of naval installations in North Vietnam. (The provocations which North Vietnam charged took place before the Tonkin incident were not given serious consideration in any of the national media.) The commitment was now definitely made, as Cronkite wrote, "to stop Communist aggression wherever it raises its head."

In 1965, American ground troops arrived in force in Vietnam and took over the burden of combat. As the nature of the war changed from a confused struggle between Vietnamese factions with outside help to a test of American military commitment, television coverage focused almost exclusively on the American effort. From 1965 to

1968, few interviews can be found with South Vietnamese military or civilian leaders, and the Vietcong and North Vietnamese were almost nonexistent on American television newscasts. As Lem Tucker, who covered the Vietnam war for NBC in 1966 and 1967, points out, "The strangest thing about the war was we never saw the enemy, the Vietcong . . . they vanished whenever we arrived." Howard K. Smith has perceptively observed about this period: "Television covered only one-third of the war—the American third."

This was not necessarily the correspondents' choice: Ron Nessen, who covered the war for NBC during this period, explained, "We were shunted by helicopter from one operation to another by military press officers who wanted to show off American initiative." With few exceptions, combat stories during this period began by showing this "initiative"—search-and-destroy patrols, landing of helicopters, air bombardments, sweeps, etc.—and concluded by measuring the effectiveness of the operation in terms of the "body count" (or what Chet Huntley called "the total score").

Next to combat stories, the most prevalent form of coverage during this period featured new types of military technology—helicopter gunships, "magic dragon" air support, Naval patrols, etc. (although the proportion of "military hardware" stories began decreasing by 1967).

There were, it also should be noted, a number of documentaries during this period that attempted to put the war in a larger perspective, such as the remarkably insightful series produced by Les Midgley for CBS. But the main impression received from the nightly dosages of regular news was one of American progress. Professor George A. Baily concluded his doctoral dissertation on the coverage of the war by network anchormen: "The results in this study demonstrate that the combat reports and the government statements generally gave the impression that the Americans were in control, on the offense and holding the initiative, at least until Tet of 1968."

The early picture of the war on television was truncated in an even more serious sense: all three networks had very definite policies about showing graphic film of wounded American soldiers or suffering Vietnamese civilians. Producers of the NBC and ABC Evening News programs said that they ordered editors to delete excessively grisly or detailed shots because they were not appropriate for a news program shown at dinnertime. A former producer of the CBS Evening News said that they also had a network policy of not showing "identifiable" American soldiers before their families were notified, and that the anchorman was supposed to warn the audience if especially "gruesome shots" were to be shown. According to former CBS News president Fred W. Friendly, these network policies "helped shield the audience from the true horror of the war." And although large numbers of Americans were wounded throughout this period, the net effect of these policies, though perhaps not intentional, was to severely restrict the coverage of wounded Americans (except in the anchormen's weekly totals).

The relative bloodlessness of the war depicted on television helps to explain why only a minority in the Harris–*Newsweek* poll said that television increased their dissatisfaction with the war. Some of the reasons given in this poll by respondents who opposed the war were "the destruction of life," "seeing wounded Americans carried out of battle" and "the horrors of war." Yet the coverage of the war by television, up until 1967, when the poll was taken, minimized American viewers' exposure to these very things. Their impression of a clean, effective technological war was, however, rudely shaken at Tet in 1968.

When large numbers of American ground troops arrived in 1965, television focused on their progress. Night after night, on all three networks, the standard scenario depicted American troops descending on an "enemy-held" area and bombarding a mostly invisible foe in the far distance; then there was a display of captured supplies or some other evidence of victory, accompanied by a tally of enemy casualties. This picture was reinforced by constant reports on the arrival of new and superior American weapons and by film, supplied by the Pentagon, which showed the bombing of the North.

Interspersed occasionally between the stories showing military progress were stories suggesting that the Americans were also rebuilding South Vietnam. For example, after showing such a story on NBC's *The Huntley-Brinkley Report,* Chet Huntley added, "The central truth of that report needs underscoring," and went on to describe the American forces in Vietnam as "builders" rather than destroyers.

There were, of course, notable exceptions to

this standard fare, but in reexamining the nightly newscasts of this period, the dominant impression is one of continuous American successes and mounting enemy losses. And therefore it is not surprising that the dominant opinion of the public during that same period was (according to the polls) one of support for the U.S. government's war policies.

The televised picture of gradual progress in the war was abruptly shattered by the Communist offensive in early 1968. On January 29, while the South Vietnamese celebrated Tet, the lunar new year, Vietcong units launched coordinated attacks on every major city in South Vietnam. The Americans suddenly found themselves besieged, and Saigon turned into a battlefield for the first time.

Whereas before Tet, television correspondents and camera crews were usually shepherded by military liaisons to preselected battle sites (and were almost entirely dependent on military transports to reach combat zones), now the military had no such control over the movements of the press. Merely by stepping outside their hotels, correspondents found themselves willy-nilly in the midst of bloody fighting. There was no way that the attacks in broad daylight on such landmarks as the Presidential palace could be concealed from television cameras.

Correspondents rushed unedited stories of desperate street fighting on the first available plane to Tokyo, where they were relayed almost instantly by satellite to the networks in New York. Rather than showing the usual carefully edited view of an orderly, controlled war, they depicted a totally chaotic situation. Instead of a constant series of American initiatives, American troops were shown on the defensive, as the Vietcong seized part of the American embassy in Saigon.

Moreover, network producers in control rooms in New York had neither the time nor the opportunity to shield American viewers from the grisly close-ups of wounded Americans, body bags, and death. On February 2, NBC News producer Robert J. Northshield was advised by Telex that an NBC cameraman in Saigon had taken "startling" color film of the offhand execution of a Vietcong officer by a South Vietnamese general, including a close-up described this way in the Telex message: "The VC falls, zoom on his head, blood spraying out." Northshield immediately telephoned the Tokyo bureau, where the film was being developed and prepared for transmission via satellite to New York, and requested that the bloody close-up be edited out for reasons of taste.

Less than ten minutes before the NBC Evening News went on the air, the edited version of the exclusive film, flashed halfway around the world by satellite, was received in New York and recorded on video tape for the broadcast. It was still "too strong," in Northshield's opinion. But there was no time for reediting the tape; all Northshield could do was order that the sequence be ended when the Vietcong officer fell to the ground.

Still, as far as Northshield could recall, "It was the strongest stuff American viewers had ever seen." And although body counts had listed hundreds of thousands of Vietcong killed in the seven-year war on television, an estimated twenty million Americans for the first time actually saw a gun pointed at a human head, then blood, and a real corpse.

For the next two months, while generals in Saigon and officials in Washington claimed a military "victory," television continued to show scenes of fighting and devastation, and openly suggested that the government statements were examples of a "credibility gap," as NBC correspondent Sander Vanocur and others put it. In his fine book *Tet,* Don Oberdorfer describes in convincing detail how the Vietcong insurgents lost virtually every battle and suffered irreplaceable losses in terms of both manpower and prestige, yet paradoxically won a decisive psychological victory in America. After witnessing on television, year after year, an almost continuous series of putative American military successes, and hearing repeated claims of a vanquished enemy emanating from Washington, the American public was unable to digest the unprecedented violence and gore they saw during Tet.

One of the most telling results of the Vietcong's psychological victory was the conversion of America's most influential newscaster, Walter Cronkite. Shocked by what he saw on television and in the screening rooms at CBS during Tet, Cronkite flew to Vietnam to personally assess the American involvement in Vietnam. A few years earlier, Cronkite had publicly supported the objectives of the war and praised the American commitment as "courageous." In the wake of Tet, Cronkite was greatly disappointed by what he saw and heard. "It was sickening to me," Cronkite is quoted by Oberdorfer as saying. "They were talking strategy and tactics with no consideration of the bigger job of pacifying and restoring the country." The "commitment . . . for a generation" he had endorsed in 1965 no longer seemed worth the price. In a CBS special broadcast on February 27, Cronkite concluded the program by calling the war "a bloody stalemate" and saying, "It is increasingly clear to this reporter that the only rational way out then will be to negotiate, not as victors but as an honorable people . . ."

The specter of an American defeat was kept before the public for the next two months by a spate of stories from Khesanh, a remote Marine base near the Laotian and North Vietnamese borders. In that February 27 special, Cronkite ominously suggested, "Khesanh could well fall, with a terrible loss of American lives, prestige and morale." The networks, especially CBS, focused on the story of besieged American Marines at Khesanh, under bombardment by the Vietcong, who were now frequently depicted as holding the initiative.

Other aspects of the situation were often neglected. Howard K. Smith of ABC bitterly complained about the networks' coverage during this period: "That terrible siege of Khesanh went on for weeks before newsmen revealed that the South Vietnamese were fighting at our side . . . and the Vietcong casualties were one hundred times ours. But we never told [the public] that. We just showed pictures day after day of Americans getting the hell kicked out of them. That was enough to break America apart."

Although in reality Khesanh never fell, and never came close to being overrun or suffering militarily the "terrible loss" that was predicted, the nightly portrayal of American soldiers on the brink of disaster apparently had its effect on public opinion. By April 1, the day that a column of American armor easily broke the "siege" of Khesanh, public opinion polls showed a dramatic deterioration of support for the war, and for the first time a majority of Americans now were opposed to the war. At almost that precise moment, President Johnson, always responsive to public opinion, announced in a moment of high drama that he would not seek a second term as President.

The Communist offensive ended at Khesanh. And the networks returned to their more routine modes of coverage—rather than using satellites, which then cost as much as $5,000 then for each feed and severely strained the limited news budgets of all three networks, filmed stories were shipped back to New York by air freight. In the first few days of Tet, ABC had used the satellite three times, NBC six times and CBS ten times; in the last six months of 1968, less than one percent of the film from Vietnam was relayed by satellite. The executive producer of ABC's evening newscast, Av Westin, advised the network's correspondents: "The satellite is simply one tool of transmission and I have decided to use it only when the expense is absolutely warranted . . . the show is running within its budget and that is achieved by making some very hard decisions on using the satellite."

The use of air freight meant that most filmed

stories would arrive in New York three to five days after they had occurred and been reported by the print media. To avoid the appearance of having stories look dated, correspondents were instructed by producers at NBC to concentrate on "timeless pieces," such as "helicopter patrols, prisoner interviews, and artillery barrages," and to "be careful" about filming events that "might date themselves." Since these procedures also allowed more time for advance screening and editing of stories, producers were again able to expunge scenes considered "too gruesome" for the dinnertime audience. And with most producers assuming that the war was now a "stalemate," correspondents were discouraged from taking excessive risks. They were told, once again, to cover "the technology of the war," as an NBC producer later described it. As in the period before Tet, the military scene was depicted as a series of orderly American actions against an unseen foe, except that now they were described in the rhetoric of stalemate, not victory.

In late 1968, Jack Fern, a field producer for NBC, suggested to Robert J. Northshield a three-part series showing that Tet had indeed been a decisive military victory for America and that the media had exaggerated greatly the view that it was a defeat for South Vietnam. The idea was rejected because, Northshield said later, Tet was already "established in the public's mind as a defeat, and therefore it was an American defeat." In a very real sense, he was correct. If the government (and networks) had not projected for years the image of invincible American progress in Vietnam, Tet might not have been viewed, with equal hyperbole, as a disastrous defeat.

Network executives often find it useful to describe their news services as "a mirror of society," since this implies that television has no choice but to reflect all that occurs within its purview. Network news, however, actually operates much more like a searchlight, which seeks out preselected targets in the dark, highlighting certain aspects of them and neglecting others.

At any given time, network producers decide what subjects will be pursued by correspondents, what particular events will be covered, what portions of a filmed story will be expurgated in the editing room, and what logic the news will be constructed on. As I point out in my book *News from Nowhere,* numerous considerations enter into these decisions and shape the picture of the news that the public sees on its television screens.

While in the early years of the Vietnam war (1964–1968), the network searchlight tended to focus on the American military initiative—troop landings, air strikes, search-and-destroy operations and awesome new military equipment being deployed—and to present a picture of slow but sure progress in the war, with the Tet offensive in 1968, the focus changed radically to stories of chaos, confusion and near collapse.

On November 1, 1968, President Johnson announced a halt to the bombing of North Vietnam and the commencement of serious negotiations aimed at peace. Accordingly, the networks again changed the focus of their coverage, this time from the battlefields in Vietnam to the negotiation tables in Paris.

At NBC, for example, producer Northshield declared that the "story" was now the negotiations, not the fighting. Although combat footage was sent to New York from the Saigon bureau every day for two months following the decision, it was aired only three times on the evening news. The preceding year, when there had been almost the same number of American combat deaths during the same period, combat stories were shown almost every night of the week. Now that the peace negotiations had become "the lead story," Northshield explained, "combat stories seemed like a contradiction and would confuse the audience."

Similar decisions were made at the other networks. The focus of network news in Vietnam was thus changed, not by the amount or quality of combat footage available (which remained approximately the same), but by the producers' decision about what the dominant story should be.

Even though the negotiations in Paris failed to produce any tangible results at that time, the actual war continued to be phased out by the networks. In March 1969, Av Westin, executive producer of the ABC Evening News, wrote to correspondents: "I have asked our Vietnam staff to alter the focus of their coverage from combat pieces to interpretive ones, pegged to the eventual pull-out of the American forces. This point should be stressed for all hands."

Then, in a Telex to ABC News' Saigon bureau, Westin informed news personnel there: "I think the time has come to shift some of our focus from the battlefield, or more specifically American military involvement with the enemy, to themes and stories under the general heading 'We Are on Our Way Out of Vietnam.' " Westin then went on to suggest the specific stories he expected the altered "focus" to produce, which included black marketing in Saigon ("Find us that Oriental Sydney Greenstreet, the export-import entrepreneur"); a newly appointed Vietnamese province chief ("Is the new man doing any better than his corrupt and inefficient predecessor?"); Vietnamese politics ("Single out the most representative opposition leader . . . and do a story centered about him"); and medical care for civilians ("Does the granddaughter sleep under the old man's bed, scrounge food for him, etc.?"). Quite predictably, ABC changed the focus of its coverage from the war itself, which was continuing unabated, with South Vietnamese casualties replacing American casualties, to human-interest stories about American disengagement and the problems it was causing the Vietnamese.

CBS and NBC also altered their coverage in late 1969 from combat pieces to stories about the "Vietnamization" of the war. Whereas President Nixon's policy of "Vietnamization" was predicated on a complex formula for gradually replacing American ground troops with an equivalent force of South Vietnamese troops, television tended to vastly oversimplify the concept. CBS, for example, filmed a ragged company of South Vietnamese soldiers training with new American weapons as an illustration of Vietnamization.

NBC, on the other hand, turned its coverage toward the periodic departure of American troops and the relinquishing of bases and equipment to the South Vietnamese.

The daily skirmishes between the South Vietnamese and the North Vietnamese were seldom the subject of film reports. An ABC correspondent pointed out that even if correspondents wanted to cover "the real war," the South Vietnamese "made it as difficult as possible." In any case, he suggested, most correspondents were under the strong impression (they "kept score" of what was actually shown on the air) that producers in New York were "not interested" in the war between the Vietnamese. (When Americans were involved, as in the battle of Hamburger Hill, the fighting was reported in terms of its futility.)

Since the main "Vietnam story" on all three networks had become in 1970 the withdrawal of American troops, the sudden invasion of neighboring Cambodia by American troops on April 30, 1970, was reported by television as a contradiction of the stated policy. Again, television viewers witnessed American helicopters, tanks, and troops striking out at an invisible enemy. This time, however, in keeping with the withdrawal theme, correspondents sought out and interviewed soldiers and pressed them for their personal feelings about the military intervention in Cambodia. Producers in New York, acutely aware of the dramatic protest in America that had closed hundreds of colleges, telecast soldiers' responses that generally showed the men's frustration with the invasion. These were juxtaposed with scenes of military advances and seemed, therefore, to undercut the official claims of a massive victory. Whether or not the victory was actually achieved, public support for the war, as measured by the polls, declined further.

Harry Reasoner later suggested, "It wasn't that television's coverage of Vietnam was inconsistent, government policy was—and television merely pointed this out." To be sure, after American forces were pulled out of Cambodia in June, television promptly returned to its routine coverage of the withdrawal story. Indeed, on reexamining the video tapes, it seems as if the withdrawal story line was never interrupted; Cambodia was simply shown as one negative portion of this long-playing story.

Television again abruptly changed the focus of its coverage in March of 1972, when North Vietnam launched a major invasion of South Vietnam. Since network crews and correspondents were severely restricted in their movements by the South Vietnamese (and were advised against taking unnecessary risks by network executives), South Vietnamese and free-lance cameramen, attached to South Vietnamese Army units, did most of the actual combat filming. The satellite was again employed to relay the scenes of battle to the American public, and since the casualties were Vietnamese, rather than American, producers made little effort to censor out the more brutal and gory moments—instead, anchormen simply warned the viewers of the violence that was to follow.

Television viewers thus saw a war that was

completely different from anything they had witnessed in the past. Scenes were frequently blurred and roughly edited (correspondents, who were not always at the scene, often had to rely on free-lance and Vietnamese army cameramen for their film). Yet they showed close-ups of fire fights, slaughters, and chaos that exceeded by far the most violent moments of Tet—bodies strewn alongside roads, entire cities leveled by artillery fire, troops fleeing in panic while officers attempted to rally them. And, after a decade of televised war, the "enemy" was finally shown. North Vietnamese tanks were knocked out, and North Vietnamese regulars were killed and captured in ambushes and running gun battles. One CBS producer commented, "For the first time, the war on television looked like a real war."

At first, as South Vietnamese bases were besieged and fell, network newsmen described each defeat as a "rout" and "disaster." Typically, after showing scenes of South Vietnamese soldiers retreating in complete disorder, the network anchormen would describe the North Vietnamese advances. By June, however, as it became clear that the South Vietnamese lines were holding, with the help of massive American bombing, the "Vietnam story" was redefined on all three networks as a hopeless stalemate.

Some seven months later, in January of 1973, the United States and North Vietnam signed a cease-fire agreement, and the networks began reassigning their correspondents and withdrawing their camera crews.

Although the lines of demarcation are sometimes incomplete—or violated by notable exceptions to the rule—television coverage still can be divided into three distinct periods, each with a dominant tone and viewpoint. Up until 1968, television coverage was controlled to a large extent by the American military, and it generally reflected a controlled American initiative which seemed to be winning the countryside and decimating the Vietcong. The searchlight rarely focused on related questions, such as the sufferings of Vietnamese civilians. Then, at Tet in 1968, the focus changed radically: Americans were shown on the defensive, endangered, and helplessly frustrated. Finally, when negotiations began at the end of 1968, television gradually changed its focus to the story of the American withdrawal.

The enormous shifts in the public's attitude, as measured by the Gallup and Harris "trend" polls, closely follow these sharp changes in television's perspective. Before Tet, a majority of Americans supported the war effort; after Tet, a majority disapproved. Certainly, there were other powerful forces at work on public opinion: newspapers, magazines, leading public figures, and the peace movement. And while network news deserves a large share of the credit for the eventual disillusionment with the war, it must also take responsibility for creating—or at least reinforcing—the illusion of American military omnipotence on which much of the early support of the war was based.

—"The Vietnam War: What Happened
  vs. What We Saw"
  TV Guide, September 29, October 6,
  and October 13, 1973.

About the Author

EDWARD JAY EPSTEIN was born in New York City in 1935. He received his B.A. and M.A. from Cornell University, his Ph.D. in political science from Harvard University, and has taught political science at Harvard and M.I.T. He is the author of *Inquest: The Warren Commission and the Establishment of Truth, Counterplot: The Garrison Case,* and *News from Nowhere: Television and the News.* He is also a frequent contributor to both *The New Yorker* and *Commentary,* and lives in New York City.

VINTAGE POLITICAL SCIENCE AND SOCIAL CRITICISM